Wellbeing for kids

Making kids smarter, happier

STAGES 4-6

Kate Daniels &
Victoria Pugh

HC CB
HARPERCOLLINS
CHILDREN'S BOOKS

First published by Collins
This edition published in India in 2024 by HarperCollins *Children's Books*
An imprint of HarperCollins *Publishers* India
Building No 10, Tower A, 4th Floor, DLF Cyber City, Phase II,
Gurugram – 122002

2 4 6 8 10 9 7 5 3 1

P-ISBN: 978-93-6569-315-7

William Collins' dream of knowledge for all began with the publication of his first book in 1819.
A self-educated mill worker, he not only enriched millions of lives, but also founded a flourishing publishing house. Today, staying true to this spirit, Collins books are packed with inspiration, innovation and practical expertise.
They place you at the centre of a world of possibility and give you exactly what you need to explore it.
Collins. Freedom to teach.

Series editor: Kate Daniels
Author: Victoria Pugh
Publisher: Elaine Higgleton
Author of the introduction: Becky Goddard-Hill
Product developer: Roisin Leahy
Development and copy editor: Jo Kemp
Proofreader: Claire Throp

Illustrations by Jouve India Ltd.
Cover design by Shamika Chaves

Typeset by Sam Vail, Ken Vail Graphic Design

Printed and bound at Nutech Print Services - India

HarperCollinsIn

Contents

Letter to Parents/Guardian 6

Stage 4

Unit 4.1: Emotions 10

Unit reflection 16

Unit 4.2: Managing my emotions 18

Unit reflection 26

Unit 4.3: Healthy body, healthy mind 27

Unit reflection 34

Unit 4.4: People in my life 35

Unit reflection 42

Unit 4.5: Respect 43

Unit reflection 50

Unit 4.6: Keeping safe 51

Unit reflection 58

Unit 4.7: Changes 59

Unit reflection 66

Unit 4.8: One world 67

Unit reflection 74

Contents

Stage 5

Unit 5.1: Loss 77

Unit reflection 84

Unit 5.2: Identity 85

Unit reflection 92

Unit 5.3: Habits to keep us healthy 93

Unit reflection 100

Unit 5.4: Me and others 101

Unit reflection 107

Unit 5.5: Love 108

Unit reflection 116

Unit 5.6: Keeping safe 117

Unit reflection 124

Unit 5.7: Changing and learning 125

Unit reflection 132

Unit 5.8: The environment 133

Unit reflection 140

Contents

Stage 6

Unit 6.1: Our emotions 143
Unit reflection 150
Unit 6.2: Healthy minds 151
Unit reflection 158
Unit 6.3: Medicines and health 159
Unit reflection 166
Unit 6.4: People and me 167
Unit reflection 174
Unit 6.5: Community and choices 175
Unit reflection 182
Unit 6.6: Our safety 183
Unit reflection 190
Unit 6.7: Tackling the tough stuff 191
Unit reflection 198
Unit 6.8: The world we live in 199
Unit reflection 206

LETTER TO PARENTS/GUARDIAN

Dear parent or guardian,

Welcome to the Collins International Wellbeing course, and the start of your child's wellbeing journey.

Collins supports this learning journey for your child through the materials in this course, and we'd like you, as parents/guardians, to be part of the experience. This letter explains how the course works, and how you can help your child to get the maximum benefit from the Collins materials.

What is the Collins Wellbeing course?

Concerns around the wellbeing of children have grown since the Covid-19 pandemic; children might have spent more time at home during the pandemic than they otherwise would have, and this has had an impact on the development of children's language and social skills, and sense of self. The Collins Wellbeing materials have been written to support parents/guardians who need to help their children navigate a world that may be unfamiliar to them, and to help support young children who need help developing their social skills, and who may be more anxious about social interactions than children used to be.

Children learn most in the first five years of life: the early years and time spent in kindergarten and nursery are recognised as the essential foundations for success at school. Millions of children will have missed out on essential formative experiences in nurseries and kindergartens because of the pandemic, and schools are now having to help children catch up. Gaps in learning – caused in this instance by the pandemic – are being recognised widely; there are similar gaps in the emotional and personal development of young children. The Collins Wellbeing course has been designed to help ensure that children are fully supported in terms of their social, personal and emotional development.

Similarly, the secondary course has been designed to support older children who have had big gaps in their social experiences of school and relationships with peers, due to the pandemic, at a formative time in their development. Our research with teachers has particularly highlighted increased anxiety in older students, especially around things like giving presentations in school, and how they manage their feelings of anxiety in different settings, and the course has been designed specifically to support that.

There is a large body of research that highlights the important benefits for children's future and achievements of focusing on wellbeing. Research suggests strong links between student wellbeing and improved academic achievement (Kirkcaldy et al., 2004; Suldo et al., 2011), while incidents of academic underachievement are associated with poorer student wellbeing (van Batenburg-Eddes & Jolles, 2013).

Other characteristics such as self-confidence and growth mindset, both of which are important for academic success, have been linked with higher student wellbeing (King, 2017), and students with lower wellbeing have been found to be at a greater risk of behavioural difficulties and school drop-out compared to their peers with higher levels of wellbeing (Arslan & Renshaw, 2018).

As such, we hope you'll agree that it is essential to support your child's wellbeing effectively.

The Covid pandemic is just one example of an event that has caused gaps in learning; this course aims to provide your children with the tools and resilience required to cope well in a range of scenarios.

Being involved as a parent/guardian

There is nothing covered in this course that should raise concerns for you. Topics covered include: identifying and managing emotions; developing healthy habits; establishing healthy relationships with peers, and how to cope when these change; being a part of a community; how to stay safe in school, at home and online; how to cope with change; and how to live sustainably and ethically.

The book that your child will be using is a workbook that they can write into, and can be used as a record of the topics they have covered, as well as something that they can refer back to in order to recap things they have learned to support their wellbeing.

Using this resource

While most of the lessons in the book will require some amount of engagement and intervention from you as the parent/guardian and will be self explanatory, there are a few chapters that will require you to be more hands-on and organize activities to drive the lesson home. Please scan this QR code to access the Wellbeing Parents' Guide, which will have detailed activities as well as lesson plans for your child.

We hope you make the most of this resource and encourage the wellbeing of your child.

Harper Collins Team

Wellbeing for kids

Making kids smarter, happier

STAGE 4

Hello and welcome to Wellbeing Stage 4!

Feelings are important

When you can talk about how you feel it is easier for other people to help you. It also helps you feel calmer and less confused.

You will be able to practise understanding and naming your feelings throughout this workbook.

It will help you learn to get on better with other people like friends or family. And it will also help you cope when things change.

Keep practising

We look after our bodies with good food and exercise, and we need to look after our minds too. That's what the activities in this book will help you do. They will help you feel more confident about yourself.

Practice makes everything easier. So, when you learn new things from this book it's a good idea to have a go at them in real life.

Self-care

As you work through this workbook you will learn some brilliant ways to take care of yourself when things feel difficult or when you try something new.

It's lovely when other people look after you and help you, but it is even better when you can do that for yourself. It's important to have some tools up your sleeve to care for yourself and know what to do when you are finding things difficult. We call that self-care.

Are you ready to learn all about it?

May your year ahead be as FANTASTIC as you are!

– Becky Goddard-Hill

Unit 4.1 Emotions

What do you know?

- What emotions do you know about?
- How do you know when you feel happy or sad?

In this unit, you will:

- Explore a range of emotion words and what they mean.
- Look at ways that your body might react when you feel different emotions.
- Discuss what it means to be resilient and reflect on your own experiences.

Lesson 1 What are emotions?

Activity 1.1a Matching emotions

Match the emotion words in the word bank to each of the pictures below.
Write the correct word on the line for that picture.

excited	shy	confused	angry	happy	scared	sad	nervous

Lesson 1 What are emotions?

Activity 1.1b Reflection

Choose two emotions (e.g. happy, excited) and reflect on a time when you have felt that way. You might like to share these examples with your family members. You can choose any emotion to reflect on.

I felt ____

when ____

____

____

____

____

____

____

____

I felt ____

when ____

____

____

____

____

____

____

____

Lesson 1 What are emotions?

Activity 1.1c Emotion log

Over the next one week, create an emotion log. At the end of each day, write about how you felt through the day.

Today I felt ______________________________

____

____

Today I felt ______________________________

____

____

Today I felt ______________________________

____

____

Today I felt ______________________________

____

____

Today I felt ______________________________

____

____

Today I felt ______________________________

____

____

Today I felt ______________________________

____

____

Lesson 2 How does my body react?

Activity 1.2a How might my body react?

Match the emotion in the left column with the physical effect it has on the body in the right column, using the examples at the bottom of the page. If you would like to share, you can put an example of when you have felt that way in the My example column.

Can you think of any other emotions and give some examples of physical effects in the empty boxes?

Emotion	Physical effect	My example
Happiness		
Fear or feeling scared		
Anger		
Sadness		

slumped posture
slow movements
tearful eyes
clenched jaw
raised voice
increased heart rate
sweating
tense muscles
smiling
relaxed muscles
feeling light

Lesson 2 How does my body react?

Activity 1.2b Emotion story

Anu is an excellent chess player, and it is also her favourite game. She's really excited for being chosen to represent her school in a chess competition.

After a week of preparations, the day of the competition has arrived.

Write a paragraph to describe how Anu might be feeling. Remember to mention the way her body is responding and how she might be feeling physically.

You can illustrate the story with a picture below.

Unit reflection

Listen to the story of *The Thing Lou Couldn't Do* here and in the bubbles, write your own reflections for each question.

1. What are emotions?

2. Think of a time when you have experienced a strong emotion. How did your body react?

3. Think of a time when you have been resilient. How did you feel at the time?

Unit 4.2 Managing my emotions

Emotion wheel

What do you know?

- Look at the emotion wheel. Are there any emotion words that are new to you?
- Choose one word from the outer wheel. Can you use it in a sentence?

In this unit, you will:

- Explore triggers for different emotions.
- Consider when behaviour is appropriate to a situation and what to do if it isn't.

Lesson 1 Why do I feel this way?

Activity 2.1 Emotion storyboard

Amit is about to leave on his first school camping trip where he will be away from home and his parents for three days. As his mother helps him pack, Amit starts feeling uneasy. What emotions do you think he might be feeling? Create a storyboard with words or pictures of what might happen next.

Lesson 2 Runaway thoughts

Activity 2.2a And Now Nobody Likes Me

Finally! I'm on the last question.... 8 X 7. What is it? Hmm...that's a hard one. It is 48? 54? 56? Ugh. I don't know. And I don't really care.

I just want to go out to play, before all the best snow is gone. Everyone else went out ages ago. They'll all be throwing snowballs and building snowmen already.

"Finish all the questions before you go out, Carrie." says Ms Ali.

I'm good at most of the multiplication tables. But the 7 times table is really hard. I don't know how anyone can work out the answers without counting on their fingers. Kesha can do it, though.

Kesha is my best friend in the whole world and she's really good at maths tables, even seven and eight.

She's really good at everything actually. And she's very funny and good at making things.

I bet she's making some good snowballs right now. I want to make some too!

"I'm just finishing the last sum, Ms Ali." I say.

I wish Kesha hadn't run out to play as soon as she was done. She would know the answer. I bet she put 58.

I'm going to put that. There...58. Finished!

Where's my coat? I can't see it. Everyone charged outside in such a hurry. I can't find it. But who cares if it's cold? There's snow to play with! Kesha and I will build a snowman together. A really big one. And make snow angels.

Right. Now I can finally go outside. Where's Kesha? We always play together at breaktime. Always. She usually waits for me and we go outside together, but I saw her run off as soon as she was finished.

Why was she in such a hurry? Was it the snow or something else? Was she trying to get away from me?

I can't see her anywhere. Is she hiding from me? I bet she is.

Lesson 2 Runaway thoughts

Activity 2.2a And Now Nobody Likes Me

How does Carrie feel in the story so far? Have you ever felt this way?

How does Carrie feel when she is finishing her work in the classroom?

What might Carrie be feeling as she gets outside?

What do you think might happen next in the story?

Lesson 2 Runaway thoughts

Activity 2.2b How to manage your thoughts

Read the information below. Have you tried any of these strategies?

What other ways could Carrie manage her emotions in this situation? What might help?

Annotate the information below with your own ideas, words or pictures to show other strategies to manage your emotions.

What can help?

Don't compare yourself to others

The key is to focus on yourself. Can you improve how you did last time in the spelling test, or can you make a new friend? Turn your envy into a goal instead.

Think it through

If you think, rather than just feel, you can put your jealousy into perspective.

You will recall that when you were younger, you got all the attention because babies are helpless and need a lot of care.

You will remember that you have other friends who you can invite too.

Don't fear missing out

Fear of missing out can make you jealous, so get rid of the fear by focusing on the good things in your life.

Maybe it's time to invite a new friend home for a meal or visit a family member?

Be a cheerleader

Say "well done" to the classmate who beat you in the test, ask your best friend how the sleepover went and offer to help out with the new baby. Don't give in to your jealousy; instead make your relationships happier and stronger.

– *Becky Goddard-Hill*

Lesson 2 Runaway thoughts

Activity 2.2c Managing my emotions

Consider strategies that might be helpful if you or a friend are having runaway thoughts. Write or draw the strategies in the trainer below.

Lesson 3 Looking after my mind

Activity 2.3 Time to relax

Think of all the ways you like to relax. Reflect on these below. What are your favourite ways to relax? Why? What else would you like to try?

Unit reflection

Consider times when you feel particular emotions. Are they primary or secondary emotions? You can use the emotion wheel to help you decide.

Write five sentences below to show some triggers for your emotions.

For example, 'When I am lonely, I feel sad.'

Emotion wheel

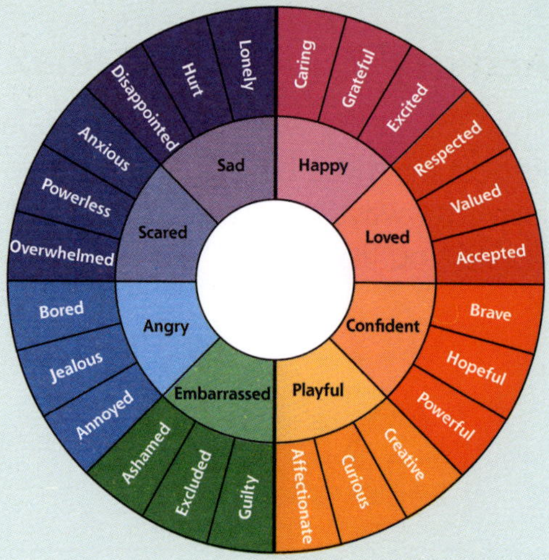

1. ______________________________

2. ______________________________

3. ______________________________

4. ______________________________

5. ______________________________

What strategies might you use to manage these emotions?

Unit 4.3 Healthy body, healthy mind

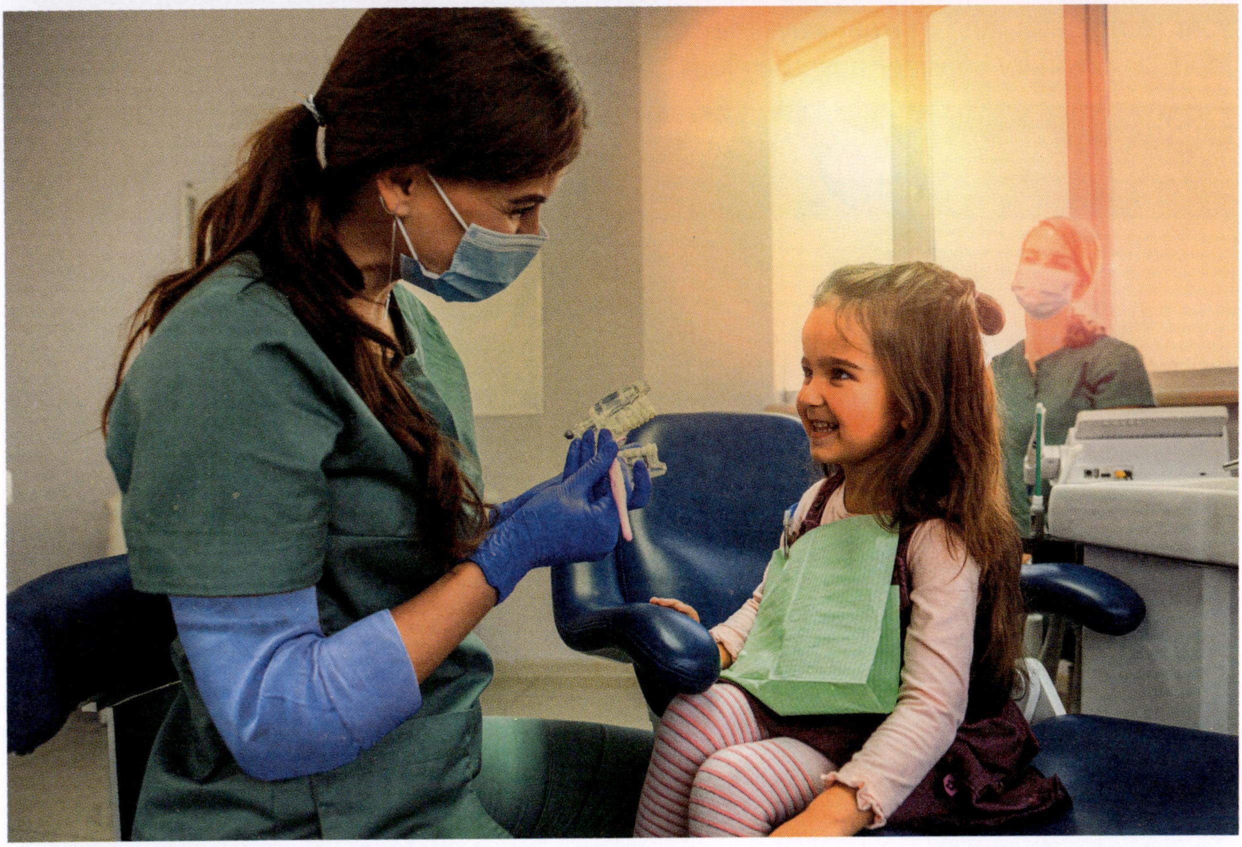

What do you know?

- What is happening in the photo?
- Have you had a similar experience to the photo?
- What does the term "healthy lifestyle" mean?
- What does "hygiene" mean?

In this unit, you will:

- Explore a range of ways to keep your body and mind healthy.
- Describe ways to ensure good oral hygiene.
- Create a balanced diet and identify key food groups.

Lesson 1 Creating a balanced meal

Activity 3.1a What do I like?

With the help of an adult, explore the variety of foods and ingredients that are present in your refrigerator, and in what ways they can be cooked and prepared. Try as many of the foods as possible. Consider how they look, taste and feel. Which foods did you enjoy?

Food	Add notes about how the food tastes or feels	Do you like it? 🙂 or ☹️

Lesson 1 Creating a balanced meal

Activity 3.1b Which food group does it belong to?

A balanced meal is one that contains all kinds of food groups in moderation for a healthy diet. Think of your daily meals and with the help of a family member, create a menu of your daily diet. Remember to pick out the key ingredients and colour-code each one to show which food group it belongs to:

blue for protein – **red for dairy** – **green for fruit and vegetables**

yellow for fats and sugars – **orange for starchy carbohydrates**

My menu

Breakfast ______________________

____

Key ingredients ______________________

____

____

____

Lunch ______________________

____

Key ingredients ______________________

____

____

____

Dinner ______________________

____

Key ingredients ______________________

____

____

____

Lesson 1 Creating a balanced meal

Activity 3.1c Nutrition information

A balanced diet helps to ensure that our body and mind receives a wide variety of vitamins, minerals and proteins. Read the information below to help you work out which food groups the foods in your menu contain. Can you make your menu even more balanced?

What foods do you enjoy from each food group?

Nutrients for a healthy mind and body

Starchy carbohydrates are a type of food that can give us lots of energy to play and have fun! They can be found in foods like potatoes, bread, rice and pasta. These foods are important because they provide our bodies with the fuel we need to run, jump, and play all day long. Starchy carbohydrates are also a good source of fibre, which helps keep us full and our digestion healthy.

Proteins are essential for a healthy body, especially for growing children. They are important for building and repairing muscles, bones and other tissues. They also help to make enzymes, hormones and other chemicals that are needed for good health. Foods that are rich in protein include meat, fish, eggs, beans, nuts and dairy products like milk and cheese. It is important to eat a variety of protein-rich foods to get all the different types of proteins that your body needs.

Dairy products, such as milk, cheese and yogurt, are an important part of a healthy and balanced diet. They are rich in calcium, which helps to build strong bones and teeth. They also contain other important nutrients like vitamin D, which helps the body absorb calcium, and vitamin B12, which is important for the nervous system. They also provide protein, which is essential for growth and development.

Fruits and vegetables are packed with nutrients that help our bodies work properly, like vitamins, minerals and fibre. They can also help protect our bodies from getting sick by boosting our immune system. Eating a variety of colours is important too, because different coloured fruits and vegetables have different nutrients. For example, orange fruits are rich in vitamin C, which helps our skin heal and fight off infections.

Some fats, like those found in nuts, seeds and oily fish, are necessary for our bodies to function properly. These healthy fats provide energy, help absorb vitamins, and protect vital organs.

Sugars, on the other hand, should be consumed in moderation, as they can cause tooth decay. Natural sugars in fruits and dairy products are a better option than added sugars found in processed foods and drinks.

Lesson 2 Looking after your oral health

Activity 3.2a Looking after my teeth

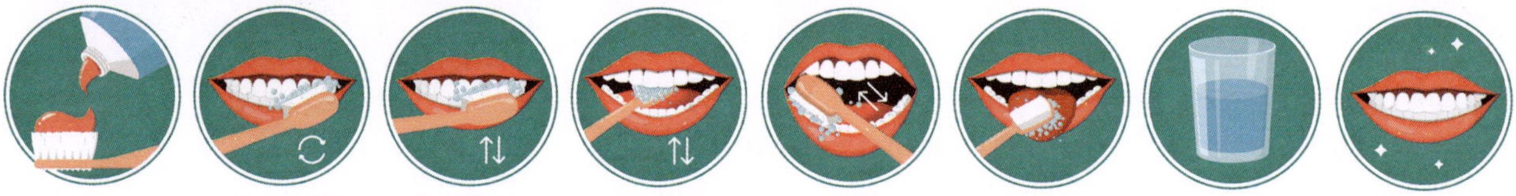

1. Why do you need to look after your teeth?

---

2. How often do you need to clean your teeth?

---

3. How long do you need to clean your teeth for?

---

4. How do you clean your teeth?

1. ______

2. ______

3. ______

4. ______

5. ______

6. ______

5. What is flossing and how do you do it?

---

6. What have you learned about how your diet can affect your teeth?

Lesson 2 Looking after your oral health

Activity 3.2b My teeth and mouth

Add labels to each part of the mouth and teeth in the diagram below.

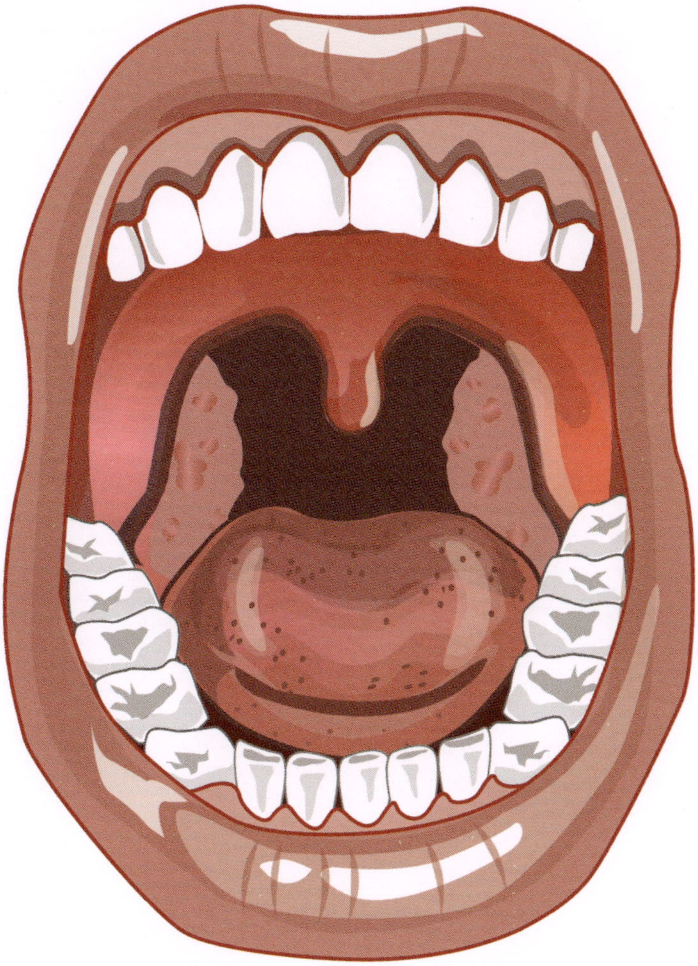

Unit reflection

Create a colourful poster which reminds other children how to keep clean and healthy. You can include all aspects of health you have learned about in this unit. You can include words and phrases too.

Unit 4.4 People in my life

What do you know?

- What do you know about relationships?
- Why do you think friendships are important?

In this unit, you will:

- Learn about different types of relationships.
- Find out why friendships are so important.
- Explore whether something fun could actually be bullying.

Lesson 1 All the people I know

Activity 4.1a Different relationships

Today you are learning about relationships. How many different relationships can you think of? Write them down, creating a web from the word 'relationships'. Don't worry, this isn't a test!

Lesson 1 All the people I know

Activity 4.1b Reflection

A relationship is a connection between two people that can be created due to either family, shared interests or work, which is held together by positive feelings. Think quietly about what you have learned about different relationships in your life.

Use this page to write or draw what you think and what you have learned.

Is there anything more you would like to know or don't understand about relationships? Write your questions here and an adult family member can answer these for you.

Lesson 2 Good friends

Activity 4.2a Different types of friends

Today you are learning about friendships. How many different types of friends can we have? Write down as many as you can think of, creating a web from the word 'friendships'.

Lesson 2 Good friends

Activity 4.2b Reflection

Think quietly about what you have learned about what makes a fantastic friend. What are the qualities about your friends that you like? What qualities would one need to be a fantastic friend?

Use this page to sketch a fantastic friend – you can label it too. Now think quietly about what you might like to introduce into your friendships following this lesson.

Is there anything more you would like to know about friendships?
Write your questions here.

____

____

Is there anything worrying you about friendships?

____

____

Lesson 3 It's only a joke!

Activity 4.3a Top five ways to help

One of the most important qualities that is required for a good relationship is respect. We love laughing and playing with our friends, but there should always be mutual respect. Teasing and bullying others shows a lack of respect for the other person. How could you help when you see someone being teased or someone being mean to another person? Write down your top five ideas.

1. ______________________________

2. ______________________________

3. ______________________________

4. ______________________________

5. ______________________________

Lesson 3 It's only a joke!

Activity 4.3b Acrostic poem

How do you think we should treat each other in our school to show respect for everyone? Arrange your ideas in an acrostic poem below. (An acrostic is a poem where each letter of a word is used to start a new line of the poem.)

R

E

S

P

E

C

T

Unit reflection

You have been asked to collect information about different relationships for a time capsule in your town. You can look back at the introduction to this unit to help you think about where you started.

Complete the sheet below to go in the time capsule with all the information you have learned.

Name: ______________________ Date: ______________________

Subject: *Everything I know about relationships*

Unit 4.5 Respect

What do you know?

- What can you see in the picture?
- Do you know what these mean?
- Why might they be used?

In this unit, you will:

- Create a rules collage.
- Hold a class debate.
- Practise your active listening skills.

Lesson 1 Rules, rules, rules

Activity 5.1 Choose the rules

Choose some rules which you have in your class or home. What could be the consequences if people didn't follow these rules?

1. *The rule* ______________________________

   ____

   If we ignored this rule the consequences might be ______________________________

   ____

   ____

   ____

2. *The rule* ______________________________

   ____

   If we ignored this rule the consequences might be ______________________________

   ____

   ____

   ____

3. *The rule* ______________________________

   ____

   If we ignored this rule the consequences might be ______________________________

   ____

   ____

   ____

Lesson 2 Different opinions

Activity 5.2a Debating points

Ask your family members to come up with a debate topic. Between yourself and a friend or sibling, pick at random two opposing views that you will be debating. Write your key points for the debate below. Remember to make them clear and concise. Use this exercise to understand how different opinions to a topic can be expressed. Everyone is a winner in this debate.

- My key argument:

- Key point 1:

- Key point 2:

- Key point 3:

- Concluding point:

Lesson 2 Different opinions

Activity 5.2b Reflect on the debate

What did you find useful about the debate? What did you find less useful?

Did it change your opinion?

Was it difficult to give your opinions when others disagree?

What have you learned?

Lesson 2 Different opinions

Activity 5.2c Voicing your opinion respectfully

It is completely normal to disagree with someone's opinions. But even a disagreement or difference of views can be shared in a peaceful, considerate and respectful manner. Write or draw three ways in which you can voice your opinion in a respectful way when you don't agree with others.

I can use my voice to...

I can be respectful by...

When I want to share my opinion, I can...

Lesson 3 Are you a good listener?

Activity 5.3a Listener's checklist

What is active listening? The cornerstone of being a good listener is to be respectful and not to interrupt when a person is speaking, and also showing interest in what they have to say. Active listening does not simply mean just hearing in silence, but also participating in the conversation that the speaker is trying to start. Observe people when they're trying to listen, and use the following chart to figure out whether they were being good listeners or not.

Your name: ______________________________

Person being observed: ______________________________

Area to observe	Outcome	Notes
Shows positive body language (leans forward and has an open manner)		
Empathises (tries to see the situation from the other person's side)		
Listens actively without interrupting		
Asks open questions		
Encourages the other person to solve their own problems		
Did they say any of these? Please circle if they did.		Tell me about... How do you feel about... On a scale of 1–10... What would you like to change? What could you do to solve this problem? What can I do to help you? I see.../Yes.../I understand... That must be hard for you. If you could wake up tomorrow and find that this problem had gone away, how would everything be different?

Lesson 3 Are you a good listener?

Activity 5.3b Being a good listener

Can you think of all the ways that being a good listener might help you in your life now and in the future? Draw or write your reflections below.

How will good listening skills help me in my life?

Unit reflection

What does respect mean to you?

Draw or write your ideas below.

How do you show respect to others?

Write three things you have learned from this unit.

1.

2.

3.

Unit 4.6 Keeping safe

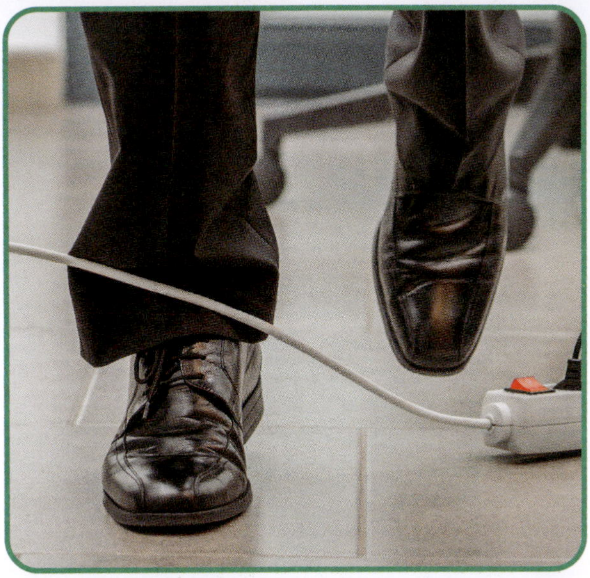

What do you know?

- What hazards can you see in the photos?
- Why do you think there are rules, regulations and restrictions online?

In this unit, you will:

- Think about how to keep safe in your day-to-day life.
- Learn about different hazards and how to keep safe.
- Think about how to stay safe online.

Lesson 1 Keeping safe around strangers

Activity 6.1a Thinking about keeping safe

You are going to be learning about keeping safe in this unit.

Let's see what you know about this subject already. List all the ways that you keep yourself safe. This can be at home, at school or out in public. How many different situations can you think of? Write these down below and discuss them with the adults in your family.

Lesson 1 Keeping safe around strangers

Activity 6.1b Places I go

Sketch a simple map of all the places you go in one week. These places might include: home, school, sports pitch, club, shops, parents'/carers' workplaces, friends' houses, playground, park, countryside. On the map, jot down the various precautions you take at the different places on it.

Lesson 2 Managing hazards

Activity 6.2 Thinking about hazards

1. A hazard is an object or a situation that can be potentially harmful and must be treated with caution at all times. Go out into your neighbourhood playground, or your school, or the kitchen at your home, and click a picture. Paste it below and circle all the possible hazards that might be there.

2. List the hazards that you have added in your picture.

3. If you were in this place, what would you do to keep yourself safe? Think about everything you have learned and write down below what you would do, or not do, to keep safe in this place.

Lesson 3 Keeping safe online

Activity 6.3a True or false

There are lots of potential harms on the internet, but there are also lots of simple things we can do online to keep ourselves safe.

Go through the true/false statements below. If you're not sure what the answer is, just go with what you think it probably is. This is not a test! It is to help you learn, and to help your adult family members to support you to keep safe online.

Statement	True or false?
Only be friends with people who you know in real life.	
Always be kind online.	
Ignore age restrictions: use any website or game for any age.	
Never share any private information online (e.g. name, address, school, phone number).	
Believe everything you read and see online.	
Share and show your parents/carers anything you are worried about online.	
Never click on any pop-ups or attachments.	
Set simple passwords.	
Never pretend to be older than you are.	
Report anything suspicious. Get an adult you trust to help you.	

Go through the answers with your guardian, then answer these questions.

1. Are there any statements in the table that you had never thought of before or that you do not understand? Write them here.

2. Is there anything you are learning about today that is worrying you? If so, talk to an adult you trust and they can help you. Write your worry below.

Lesson 3 Keeping safe online

Activity 6.3b Reflection

Add some bullet points below about what you have learned about online safety.

Is there anything you need to do or learn more about? (Please include as much detail as you can so that your guardian can help you.)

Do you need help with anything from a trusted adult? If so, can you explain what help you would like?

If you are worried about anything you have learned in this lesson, make sure you talk to an adult you trust so that they can help you.

Unit reflection

Thinking about the hazards and dangers you have been learning about, draw a picture of yourself putting the safety measures covered in this unit in place.

How many can you add? You can circle these safety measures and label them if you feel this will make them clearer.

Unit 4.7 Changes

What do you know?

- What do you know about the value of mistakes?
- What do you think 'thinking about your thinking' means?

In this unit, you will:

- Explore changing friendships.
- Consider how, from different perspectives, mistakes may not be all they seem.
- Learn how to watch your thoughts.

Lesson 1 When friendships change

Activity 7.1 What I have learned

Change is inevitable. While growing up is a visible way in which people change, there are other kinds of changes too, which might result in a difference of opinion or even disagreements. But just because people change or disagree, it doesn't mean that their relationships have to end. Speak to your guardian about how they dealt with changes and how they manage disagreements. Use this Venn diagram to consider all that you have learned about how to deal with changes and disagreements in relationships.

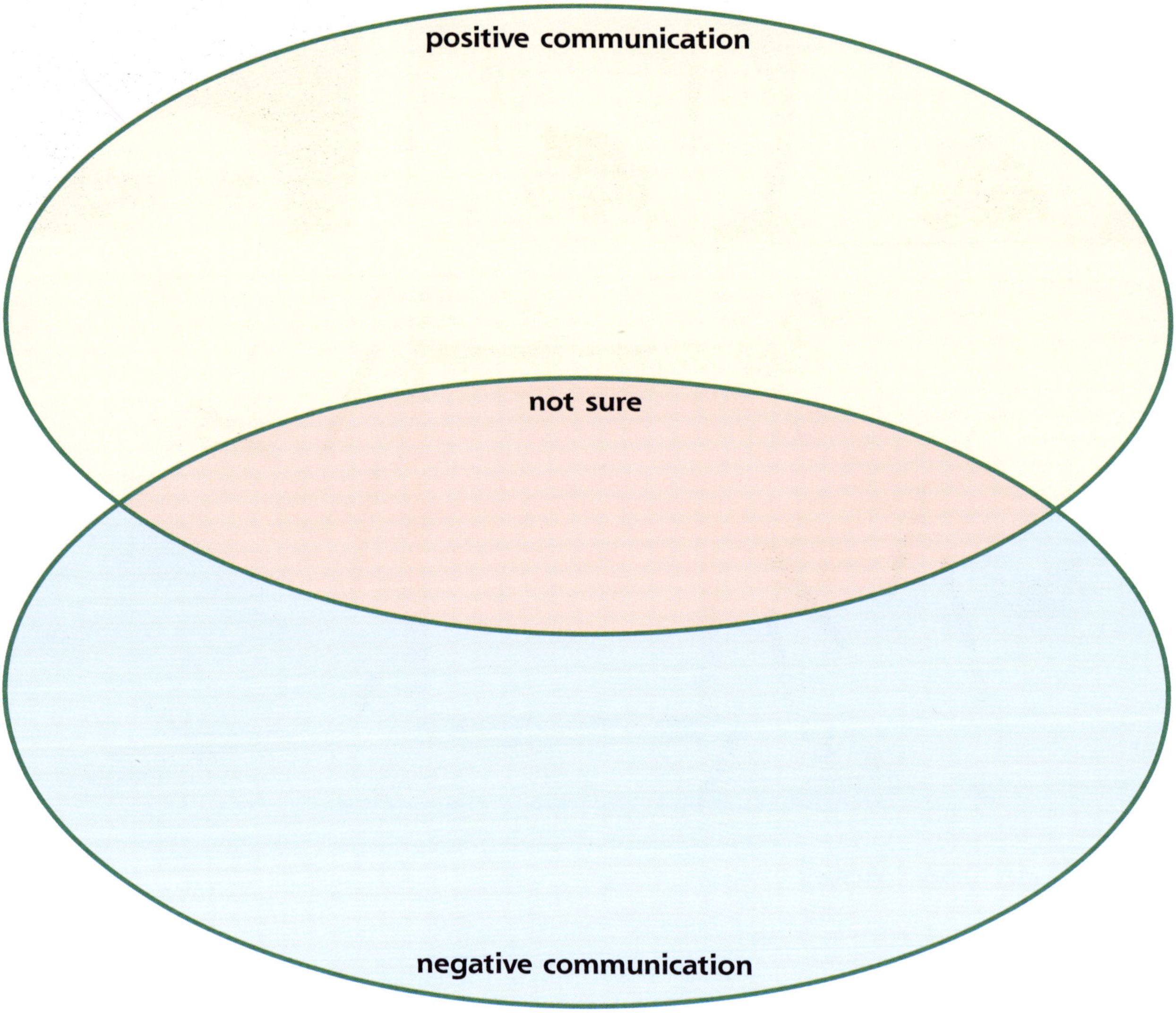

Write down one strategy which you feel would be useful in the future when dealing with friendship disagreements, and one strategy for how to seek help and get the support you need when friendships change.

1. ______________________________

2. ______________________________

Lesson 2 Mistakes

Activity 7.2a What I think of mistakes...

Write or doodle your thoughts about mistakes on this page.

For example, what do you think of others making mistakes? What do you think of yourself when you make mistakes? Do you think mistakes are good or bad or both? Why? Discuss your thoughts with a family member or friend.

Lesson 2 Mistakes!

Activity 7.2b Leo's story

Leo was an artist who lived high up in a little village in the hills.

Along with growing vegetables, he had sketched and drawn with pencils since he was a little boy.

He loved to watch the sky, the moon and the sun, the shadows and the seasons. He always noticed things around him, often little things that other people did not.

The villagers would come to him to ask if he could draw a picture for them to send to a relative far away.

'He's so talented,' they would say.

This was the way it was and the way it had always been with Leo, but one evening as he was tidying up his little home, he realised that every single picture he had ever drawn was grey. It hit him, just like that!

He looked out of his window and noticed, as he always did, all the beautiful colours around him and suddenly, just like that, he made a promise to himself that from now on he was going to use colour – he was going to learn to paint!

The very next day, he set off to the nearest town and returned with brushes and canvases and with tubes of paint in every colour you could imagine!

He set straight to work, sitting on the edge of his field overlooking the valley. He painted the sky and the trees and the people working in their fields, the birds, the flowers, on and on.

Finally, as the light was fading, he stepped back from his work to see how it looked ... and it looked AWFUL!

None of the colours looked real; there were brushstrokes and paint runs.

When the villagers saw it, they all said, 'Oh dear! He's made a big mistake; he should stick to what he's good at.'

But Leo would not give up. Every day he went out and painted and painted and painted. But he didn't feel happy with his work.

One evening, a friend came to see him and Leo told him about his mistake – the money and time he had wasted at something he would never be good at.

'I'll just go back to drawing,' he said. 'I know I can do that.'

'Wait, let me see your work,' said his friend.

When he saw it he was amazed. 'This is incredible, Leo!'

'Don't tease me!' said Leo.

'No, I mean it! Your work is unique and intriguing. I love it! You need to change your perspective. Your mistake is a gift – for where there is grey, you now have colour!'

Answer these questions, thinking back to Leo's story.

1. Why do you think the villagers thought Leo had made a mistake?

2. Why did Leo think he had made a mistake?

3. What did Leo's friend see that everyone else hadn't?

4. Do you think Leo made a mistake or not? Why?

5. How can this story help you to think more positively about your mistakes?

Lesson 3 Think about your thinking

Activity 7.3a

Metacognition is a big word, but it is necessary to understand. It means thinking about the ways in which we think about things. Metacognition helps us examine our thinking and how we can improve it by recognising the patterns in the way we generate ideas. Try thinking about your thinking with these questions.

1. When does your brain do its best thinking?

2. What helps you?

3. How do you manage your thinking?

Lesson 3 Think about your thinking

Activity 7.3b Visualisation

One of the tools that helps us think better and generate new ideas is visualisation. Simply put, visualisation is when we make pictures in our minds. These can be used for studying, learning about how we think and also for relaxation. Read and follow the visualisation exercise below.

Sit comfortably with your back straight against the chair, with both feet on the ground, your hands on your lap and your eyes gently closed.

Become aware of sitting in your chair and then take your awareness to your breathing – notice how air goes in and out of your body. Listen to this and feel it go in and out.

Breathe comfortably and slowly and count your breath in and out.

Thoughts might come into your head. If this happens or your mind wanders, simply bring your thinking back to your breathing.

Now imagine a television screen in front of you. On the screen you can see a bright blue sky on a sunny day.

There are fluffy white clouds floating across the sky and the air is warm.

You feel really calm and happy.

You realise that all the fluffy clouds are your thoughts and if you listen really carefully you might even be able to hear them.

Whether you hear your thoughts or not, just let them drift past you on the clouds and float away across the blue sky and off the screen.

Watch the clouds float past for a while, seeing your thoughts come and go.

When you feel ready, open your eyes and have a good stretch.

Reflection on the visualisation

How did that visualisation feel?

____

What did you notice about your thoughts?

____

Was there anything you really liked about it?

____

Was there anything you found hard?

____

Unit reflection

Friendship issues, making mistakes and thinking can all be hard work! Can you list one thing from each lesson that you are going to practise? Write them down here.

1. ____

2. ____

3. ____

Sometimes it's good to find a way to relax and switch off our thinking and our actions and simply enjoy 'being' and finding our calm centre.

Here is a visualisation for you to learn. Once you have got the hang of this, you can use it any time to calm your mind and centre yourself.

A feeling of calm

Your mind is very powerful, and your imagination has the power to help you relax.

Think about the feelings in your body right now – are any of your muscles tense or uncomfortable? Think about each part of your body. Start at the top of your head and scan down over your face, your torso, your arms and legs, all the way to your toes.

As you breathe in, imagine you are breathing in the feeling of calm.

As you breathe out, imagine you are breathing out any feelings of tension or anxiety.

– Poppy O'Neill

Unit 4.8 One world

What do you know?

- What does this Indigenous American proverb mean to you? Discuss it with the adults in your family:

  We do not inherit the earth from our ancestors (people who came before us). We borrow it from our children.

In this unit, you will:

- Learn about the 4 Rs.
- Take a look at some of the issues around plastic pollution.
- Understand the 30 human rights.

Lesson 8.1 Reduce, recycle, reuse, repurpose

Activity 8.1 Planning a persuasive letter

Write a letter to your headteacher or school governors, explaining the importance of the 4 Rs: Reduce, Recycle, Reuse, Repurpose. Think about how best to explain what the terms mean, give examples of ways in which the school can encourage them and point out the benefits to the school and the environment. Plan the key points you want to include in each section.

Introduction

Reduce

Recycle

Reuse

Repurpose

Conclusion

Lesson 8.2 How does plastic affect our planet?

Activity 8.2a My pledge

In these images we see what happens when we use plastic bottles once and don't recycle. Unlike natural substances like wood and paper, plastic takes a lot longer to be broken down by nature, and therefore tends to accumulate and pollute if not recycled or reused. What can you do to change this?

We all have the power to make change for the better…

I pledge ____

____

____

____

____

Lesson 8.2 How does plastic affect our planet?

Activity 8.2b Plastic and our planet

Read this information about plastics to learn more and then answer the questions.

All about plastic

Plastic is made using oil, gas or coal. Scientists discovered how to make the first plastics in the nineteenth century.

Plastics are a very versatile material which has become widely used for a huge variety of purposes due to it being waterproof, flexible, adaptable and cheap to make.

The biggest drawback, however, is the cost to the planet. Plastic is not biodegradable, which means that it cannot be broken down naturally and will take centuries to break up and disappear.

Plastic can end up in rivers, the sea and other waterways, causing pollution and danger to wildlife, which can get caught up in it or eat it by mistake.

Because it doesn't biodegrade, it can float in the sea for many years and get carried around the globe by the sea's currents. As a result, there are now huge patches of plastic floating in the some of the world's oceans.

1. Why are plastics so popular?

2. What is the main drawback of plastic?

Lesson 8.3 Human rights

Activity 8.3 The 30 human rights

Read the information below to learn about the 30 different human rights.
An article is a separate paragraph or note outlining one of the rules.

Article 1 Everyone is born free and deserves equal rights.	**Article 2** Everyone has basic human rights regardless of their differences.	**Article 3** Everyone has the right to live, be free, and be safe.
Article 4 No one should be held as a slave.	**Article 5** No one should be tortured or be treated as less than human.	**Article 6** Everyone has the right to be recognised as a person no matter where they are.
Article 7 Everyone should be treated as equal by the law.	**Article 8** The law should protect anyone whose rights have been violated.	**Article 9** No one should be arrested, placed in prison or exiled without a legitimate reason.
Article 10 Everyone has the right to a fair trial by a fair court.	**Article 11** Everyone should be considered innocent until they are proven guilty of a crime. Penalties must be fair.	**Article 12** Everyone has the right to privacy and their reputation.
Article 13 Everyone has the right to travel freely.	**Article 14** Everyone can escape to another country if they are seeking asylum from persecution in their country.	**Article 15** Everyone has the right to choose and maintain the country of their nationality.
Article 16 Everyone has the right to get married and build a family. Both partners have equal rights.	**Article 17** Everyone has the right to own property. No one should have their property taken away without reason.	**Article 18** Everyone has the right to choose or change their religious beliefs.

Article 19 Everyone has the right to express their opinion and to receive information through any media.	**Article 20** Everyone has the right to assemble peacefully.	**Article 21** Everyone has the right to participate in their government and elect officials.
Article 22 All members of society have a right to social security.	**Article 23** Everyone has the right to fair working conditions, fair salary, equal pay for equal work, and the right to form and join trade unions.	**Article 24** Everyone has the right to reasonable work hours, including periodic holidays with pay and the right to rest and leisure.
Article 25 Everyone has the right to adequate living conditions, food, health care, and security in the event of circumstances beyond their control.	**Article 26** Everyone has the right to a good education.	**Article 27** Everyone has the right to participate in community cultural activities and to share in scientific advancements.
Article 28 Everyone is entitled to a society in which the rights and freedoms of this declaration can be fully realised.	**Article 29** It is our responsibility to protect the rights of others.	**Article 30** Your human rights can never be taken away.

Which human right, or human rights, do you think are most important and why?

____

____

____

____

____

____

____

Unit reflection

Consider what you have learned across this unit. Write or draw your new knowledge below.

What are the three most interesting things you have learned?

1. ____

____

2. ____

____

3. ____

____

Do you have any questions or anything else you now want to learn more about?

____

____

____

Wellbeing for kids

Making kids smarter, happier

STAGE 5

Hello and welcome to Wellbeing Stage 5!

All feelings matter

As the new school year starts, we hope you feel confident and excited about the year ahead.

But don't worry if you feel a bit nervous too – that's okay. We all have a mix of feelings every single day.

This workbook aims to help you express and understand all your feelings. It is also packed with ways to help you feel better when you find life hard. There are so many things you can do to help yourself.

A strong mind

When you exercise your body through running and swimming, it gets stronger. When you exercise your mind, it gets stronger too.

Working through this workbook will help you feel more in control of your feelings and more confident about yourself.

Yes you can

As you work through this workbook you will learn some awesome things, such as:

- how to understand your feelings
- how to be a good friend
- how to keep safe

and all sorts of other helpful ways YOU CAN look after yourself and make life better.

It is amazing what you can do when you know how.

Are you ready to give it a go?

May your year ahead be as amazing as you are!

– Becky Goddard-Hill

Unit 5.1 Loss

What do you know?

- What can you see in the pictures?
- Have you ever been in this situation?
- How did you feel?

In this unit, you will:

- Consider how people feel when they experience the loss of a person they love.
- Research the ways in which different cultures and religions celebrate a person's life when they have died.

Lesson 1 Losing something

Activity 1.1a Storyboard

Create a scenario where someone has lost something. Draw a picture of each freeze frame. Write a sentence to explain what is happening in the scene, then use key words or phrases to explain how each of the characters is feeling. Discuss the scenario with an adult in your family.

Lesson 1 Losing something

Activity 1.1b Emotion strategies mind map

Think about the ways in which you might be able to overcome some of the emotions that you experience when you lose something and can't get it back. For example, if you lose something that belongs to someone else you could apologise. Annotate the box below with examples of strategies and discuss them with your friends and family members.

What could I do?

Lesson 2 Losing someone we love

Activity 1.2a People you love

Think of some people you love in your life. What are your favourite things to do with them? How do you like to spend time together? Write down or draw some of the things you enjoy doing together below.

Lesson 2 Losing someone we love

Activity 1.2b Reflection

Sit with your guardian or parent and discuss what it means to lose someone close to you. Ask them how they dealt with grief. Remember that losing people and changing through loss is a part of life. If you ever feel big emotions or feelings coming when you think about these topics, talk to an adult in your family about it. Write three key things you have learned.

1. ______________________________

____

____

____

2. ______________________________

____

____

____

3. ______________________________

____

____

____

Who or where could you go for support following loss/change?

____

____

____

____

What advice would you give to support a friend who has undergone a loss or a big change? Feel free to go online and look for appropriate resources that can help you.

____

____

____

____

____

Lesson 3 Celebrating life in different cultures

Activity 1.3a Changes in our lives

What comes to mind when you think of the word 'change'?

Use the space below to create a mind map of everything you can think of regarding change in your life, in other's lives or in life around you.

Lesson 3 Celebrating life in different cultures

Activity 1.3b Reflection

Did you know that in Mexico, people hold celebrations to honour and remember their friends and loved ones they have lost? They prepare their loved ones' favourite foods and decorate their graves. Held in early November, Dia de los Muertos, or the Day of the Dead, is full of colour and happiness, as people celebrate the lives of those who have departed. Look up with an adult about this vibrant event online.

List three things you have learned today about celebrating life around the world.

1. ______________________________

2. ______________________________

3. ______________________________

How is life celebrated in your own culture or religion?

Unit reflection

Think about what you have learned in this lesson and then write your own definitions of these words.

Grief – ____

____

____

____

____

____

Loss – ____

____

____

____

____

____

Celebration – ____

____

____

____

____

____

Love – ____

____

____

____

____

____

Unit 5.2 Identity

What do you know?

- What do you think is happening in the photo?
- How might the children be feeling?
- What is the child in the middle of the photo holding?

In this unit, you will:

- Consider why you are special and what you have achieved.
- Create your own edited photos.
- Explore a range of strategies to look after your mind.

Lesson 1 Celebrating achievements

Activity 2.1a My achievements

Think about something you are proud of or something you have achieved, and why you are proud of it.

Describe the achievement below. You can illustrate it if you would like to.

I am proud of ____

Lesson 1 Celebrating achievements

Activity 2.1b What types of achievements do people celebrate in life?

Work on your own or with a family member to draw and label achievements that people might celebrate.

Lesson 2 Images on the internet

Activity 2.2a Before and after pictures

Stick in your 'before' photo and then the edited 'after' photo.

Annotate all of the changes you made. Why did you make these changes?

Lesson 2 Images on the internet

Activity 2.2b How to support your positive self-esteem

After photoshopping the image in the exercise before, think about how many images are there on the internet. Are all of them true? Sometimes, we might look at photos online and compare ourselves to the person or thing represented. Even though the images might be photoshopped, it might not appear so to us, and we might end up judging others and ourselves from it and end up experiencing negative emotions. But that would be incorrect. What strategies can you think of to use to support your self-esteem and remind yourself how fantastic you are? Talk to an adult family member about it and write your ideas to create a mind map below.

Lesson 3 Self-care

Activity 2.3a What is self-care?

What does self-care mean? Note your ideas in the balloons below. You can write sentences or words, or draw pictures you associate with self-care. Get a friend or sibling to do the same exercise and compare how different or similar their ideas of self-care are.

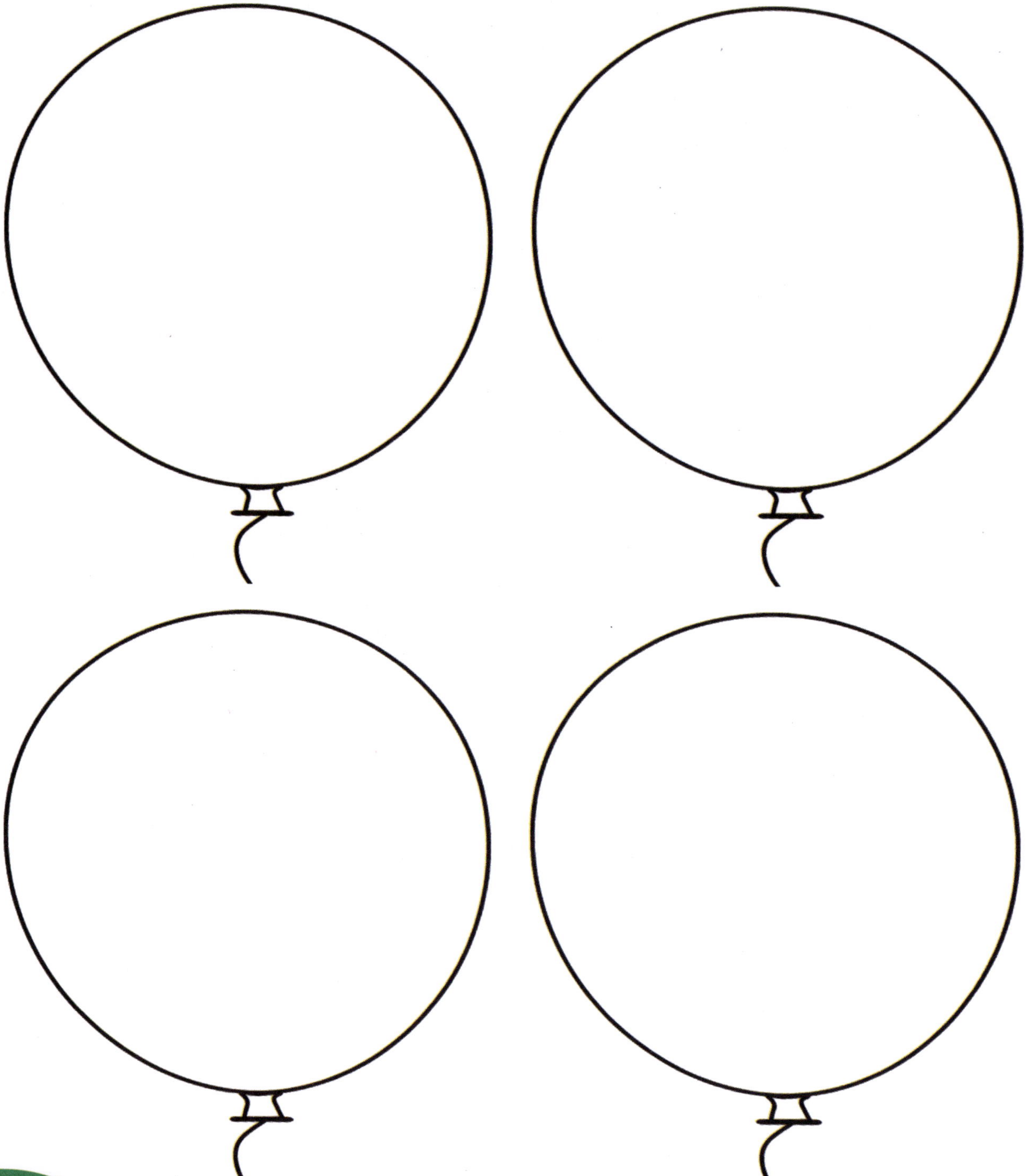

Lesson 3 Self-care

Activity 2.3b Keeping healthy

Think about all the ways you keep your body healthy and write them in the left-hand circle below. Now think about any ways you can keep your mind healthy and write them in the right-hand circle. If any are for both a healthy body and mind, write them in the middle where the two circles overlap.

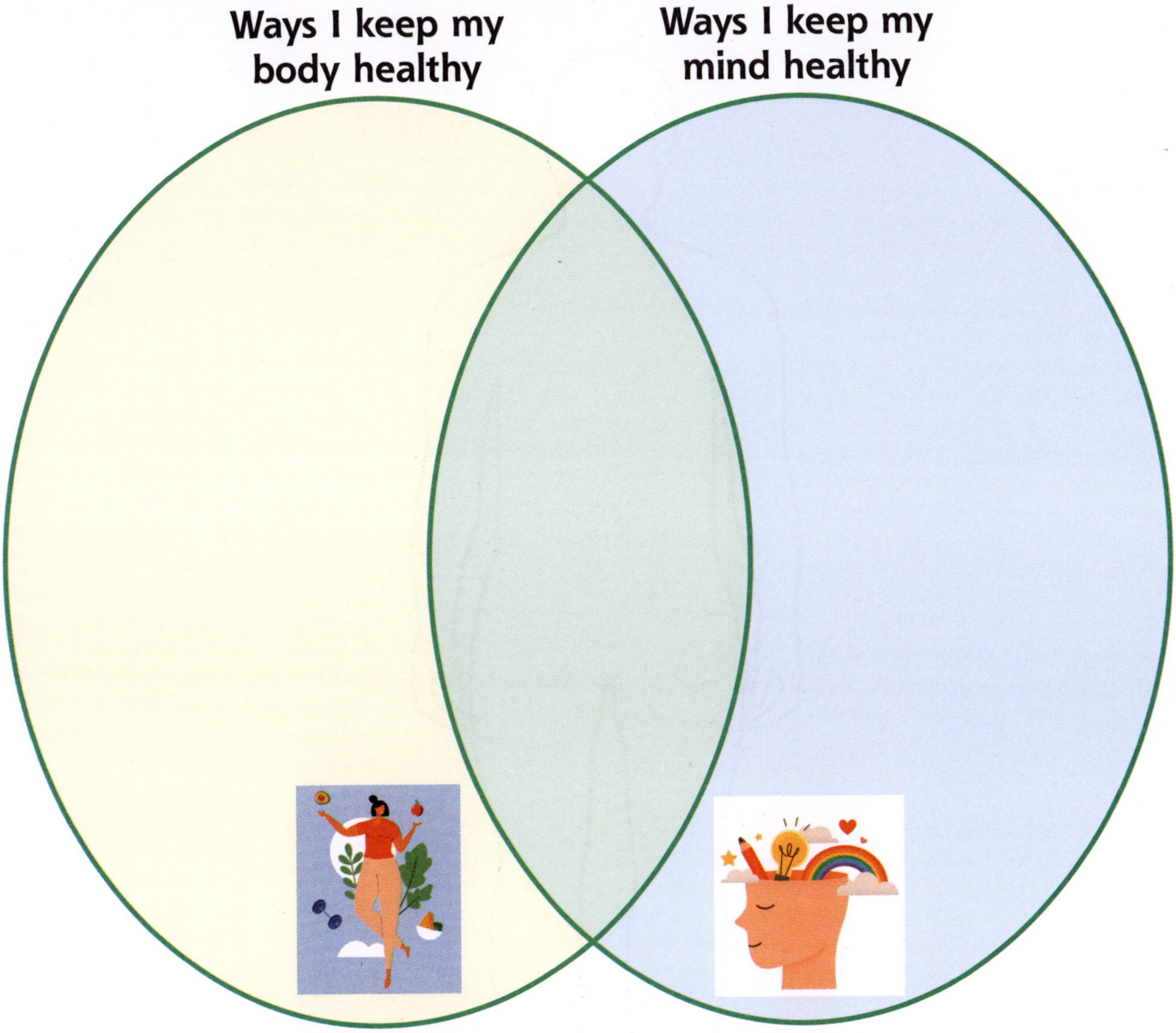

Have you written anything in the section where the two circles overlap? Which things work for both body and mind?

____

____

____

Unit reflection

What makes you, you?

Think about all of the things which make you who you are and write them around or inside the outline below.

Think about the roles you play with other people and the things you do. For example, you might be a big brother, a caring daughter, a talented chef or a fast runner. Don't forget to decorate the person below to look like you!

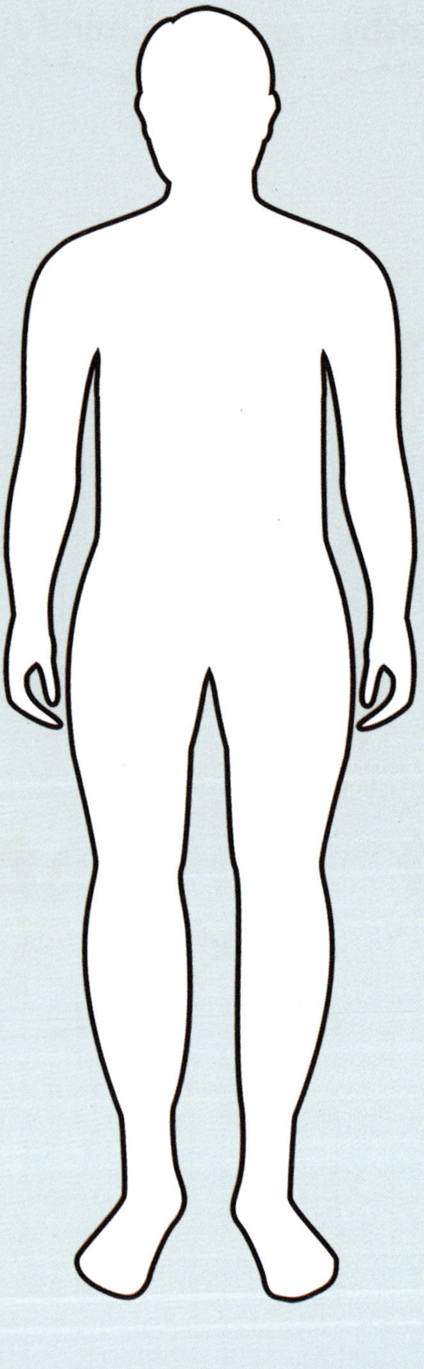

Unit 5.3 Habits to keep us healthy

What do you know?

- What are the people in these photos doing?
- Why might they be doing these things?

In this unit, you will:

- Learn about the importance of sleep.
- Find out what can help you to sleep better.
- Learn about the importance of sunlight, vitamin D and exercise for good physical and mental health.

Lesson 1 Time to sleep!

Activity 3.1a Sleep, sleep, sleep

Why might children like or dislike bedtime? Use the mind maps below to record your thoughts.

Dislike

Like

Lesson 1 Time to sleep!

Activity 3.1b Wordsearch

Can you find all the words in the box, which link to how you might feel if you don't get enough sleep?

f	o	r	g	e	t	f	u	l	n	e	s	s	w
a	x	s	o	f	o	w	o	j	t	x	l	c	i
t	y	r	k	e	y	g	u	n	s	h	e	q	n
i	a	m	d	d	h	r	h	h	g	a	e	u	a
g	s	j	w	h	n	u	g	e	a	u	p	v	t
u	g	y	o	e	r	m	u	n	s	s	y	z	t
e	a	u	g	a	a	p	v	d	k	t	b	w	e
h	f	r	t	d	c	y	a	w	n	i	n	g	n
t	i	m	p	a	t	i	e	n	t	o	m	p	t
h	y	g	s	c	y	a	p	g	r	n	j	l	i
s	e	s	h	h	i	z	s	c	a	k	v	b	o
h	q	j	c	e	m	o	t	i	o	n	a	l	n
s	c	o	b	s	r	m	s	u	f	q	y	w	g

Forgetfulness	**Impatient**
Yawning	**Fatigue**
Headaches	**Inattention**
Sleepy	**Grumpy**
Emotional	**Exhaustion**

Lesson 1 Time to sleep!

Activity 3.1c Why is sleep important?

List four reasons why sleep is important. Try finding more reasons by looking up online or asking the adults in your family.

What is the difference between rest and sleep?

Lesson 2 Getting to sleep

Activity 3.2a Bedtime routines

In the table below, write your current bedtime routine and the times that each part happens. There may be some days which are different and that is ok.

Time	Activity	Detail	How effective is this to help you to get to sleep?

What would you like to change about your current routine?

____

____

____

____

Lesson 2 Getting to sleep

Activity 3.2b Top five tips for an effective bedtime routine

Can you share your top five tips for creating an effective bedtime routine? Ask your friends for their top tips too.

Top 5 list

1 ______________________________

2 ______________________________

3 ______________________________

4 ______________________________

5 ______________________________

Lesson 3 Exercise and natural light

Activity 3.3 Exercise and vitamin D

Using a range of online sources and books from your library, research one of the following areas:

- Why vitamin D is important and how we can get more vitamin D.
- Why exercise is important for our body and mind.

Don't forget to record where you found the information so that you can check that they are reliable sources. Share this information with the adults in your family too.

Information found	Source

Unit reflection

Consider what you have learned about the importance of good sleep, natural light and regular exercise to your physical and mental health. Write or draw your answers around the cloud to create a mind map.

Key things I have learned about the importance of sleep and exercise

Unit 5.4 Me and others

What do you know?

- Why and how might relationships with friends and family change?
- How would you support a victim of bullying?
- Look at this picture. What does it mean to you? How could it relate to you and your family, friends or classmates?

In this unit, you will:

- Learn about different households.
- Understand changes in friendships.
- Consider how to support victims of bullying.

Lesson 1 Our families

Activity 4.1a My family

Sketch a picture of your family in the frame below. Put everyone in the picture: your family/people you live with, including any extended family or other people who live in your house. If possible, copy this page and get your friends to do the same activity. Then, in pairs, interview your friend about your drawing, and notice the ways in which their and your family are same or different.

Notes: Some interesting things about my family/people I live with (for example, hobbies, beliefs, customs, jokes, favourite food).

Lesson 1 Our families

Activity 4.1b Reflection

What new things have you learned about your friends? How did learning these new things make you feel?

Lesson 2 Different friendships

Activity 4.2a My friendship map

Imagine your life as a path, from when you were born to how old you are now. Draw this path from the top to the bottom of this page. Then think about the friends you have had in your life and draw these friends on to your path. You don't have to draw all of them, just the ones who have been closest to you (you can just draw them as stick people or simple figures). Beside them, write their name and roughly how old you were when you met them.

Lesson 2 Different friendships

Activity 4.2b Reflection

1. What have you learned in this lesson?

2. Think about your friendships now and since you were very little. How have they changed? How does this make you feel?

3. How might they change in the future? How does this make you feel?

4. Is there anything you would like to find out more about or that you are worried about?

Lesson 2 Different friendships

Activity 4.2c Making friends

Read these two extracts from Ammar's story in *The New Kid* and think about the different ways we make friends.

Everyone seemed to know each other well here. As the children chatted, Ammar felt even lonelier than he did at home. He wished he was at school in Syria with his best friend, Omar, playing football together in the playground.

The teacher said something, and everyone turned to Ammar. Ammar didn't understand what she'd said, so he stared at his shoes. He wanted to run and hide in the toilets, but he didn't even know where they were!

Later...

Ammar jumped when he felt a hand on his shoulder.

It was Tom. "You're really good at tennis!" he said. "Let's go and play! Come on!"

Had Ammar heard right? Did Tom say he was good? Ammar knew what that meant!

Tom put out a hand to help Ammar up and smiled. He said something else that Ammar couldn't understand, but it didn't matter. Ammar could tell he was being a good friend.

Lesson 3 Being a bystander

Activity 4.3 How to be an active bystander

Look carefully at the image above. What do we mean by bullying? And what are the different ways that people can bully others? Is it only face to face, or can it happen online too? And is it limited to just physical and verbal bullying, or are there more ways? Can you label the victim, the bystander and the person/people doing the bullying? How do you think the person is being bullied here?

How could the bystander in this picture help the victim safely? What does it mean to be an active bystander? List all the different ways you can think of and ask your guardian for their tips too.

Is there anything that has worried you in this lesson or that you would like to know more about?

Unit reflection

Think about all that you have learned and explain all the different ways you can be a better friend, family member and member of society.

-
-
-
-

Unit 5.5 Love

What do you know?

- What can you see in the picture?
- What do you think the heart symbolises?
- How do people express love?

In this unit, you will:

- Identify people that you love in your life.
- Create a family activity jar.

Lesson 1 Love is all around

Activity 5.1a Love, love, love

Who do you love? You can draw pictures or write in the hearts. Remember, they do not have to be family.

Lesson 1 Love is all around

Activity 5.1b Planning acts of love and kindness

Think of the people you love. Have you noticed that different people express love in different ways? Some people prefer hugs, while some don't. Different relationships also call for different ways of expressing love. So how about you plan on your act of love taking into consideration who you want to show it to? Who are you planning to show an act of love and kindness to?

What do they like and dislike?

What will you do?

How do you think they will respond?

Lesson 2 Spending time together

Activity 5.2 Family activities

Draw or write about a time when you have enjoyed an activity with your family or people you love.

What made the activity so fun? How did you feel when you spent time with your family?

Lesson 3 Being part of a community

Activity 5.3a Kindness in my community

Get your friends together and consider what projects you could carry out to spread kindness within your community. Remember to listen to all of the ideas in your group and then decide on one to plan.

What we are going to do ______________________________

____

____

____

____

____

____

____

____

Why ______________________________

____

____

____

____

____

____

What we will need and who will get it.

How long it will take

Our plan

Lesson 3 Being part of a community

Activity 5.3b Reflection

Reflect on what you think community means. Add words or phrases which you think are relevant to community to make a mind map below.

What is a community?

Unit reflection

Consider the following statements. Do you agree or disagree with them? Put a mark on the scale to show how you feel about each statement. Then write any comments or thoughts you have on the statement below.

1. Your friends and family can help you when you are feeling low or sad.

Strongly agree **Strongly disagree**

2. Spending time with people you care about is important.

Strongly agree **Strongly disagree**

3. Helping others can support your own wellbeing.

Strongly agree **Strongly disagree**

Unit 5.6 Keeping safe

What do you know?

- Where are the different places you go to online and how do you keep yourself safe there?

In this unit, you will:

- Find ways to stay safe online.
- Consider how to keep safe in extreme weather and find out why this is becoming more common.
- Find ways to stay safe when gaming.

Lesson 1 Think before you chat

Activity 6.1a Dangers online

Here are some of the main dangers online. Go through these and rank their seriousness in terms of how dangerous you think they could be from 1 to 10 (with 10 being the most serious). Give your reasons in the final column.

If you are not sure, just go for what you feel is right – your guardian will go through these with you when you have finished.

Situation	Seriousness (from 1 to 10)	Reason
Sharing your passwords		
Posting things you wouldn't want adults in your life to see		
Clicking on email or message links		
Talking to and trusting people you meet online		
Not covering up your webcam		
Misinformation or fake news		
Sharing or showing personal information		

Lesson 1 Think before you chat

Activity 6.1b Reflection

Reflect on what you have learned in this lesson by answering this question:

How can I keep safe when talking to people online?

You can write your thoughts as bullet points, a mind map or a doodle if you wish, as long as it is easy to understand!

Has anything worried you in this lesson? Talk to your adult family members about any worries you might have.

____

____

____

Is there anything more you would like to know or anything you don't understand?

____

____

Lesson 2 It's so hot! It's so cold!

Activity 6.2a Staying safe in the hot and the cold

Have you ever experienced extreme heat or extreme cold? Think about the last time you experienced extreme weather. What did you do to stay safe then?

Talk to your family members about how to recognize bad weather and what precautions to take in order to remain safe. Draw a person in each bubble.

In one bubble it is a very hot day and the person is ready to stay safe in the heat.

In the other bubble it is a very cold day and the person is ready to stay safe in the cold.

Think about everything you have learned and supply them with everything they will need. You can label your picture too.

Lesson 2 It's so hot! It's so cold!

Activity 6.2b How we affect the climate and how the climate affects us

Here is some information from a book called *Climate Change: Heatwaves and Big Freezes*. Read the text, then write down what you understand about the changing world temperatures.

You can also use this space to tell your guardian if there's anything you want more information on.

In the last 120 years, the human population has grown five times larger. To house and feed everyone, many forests have been cut down to build more factories, farms and cities. Billions of humans working, playing and travelling has resulted in more fossil fuels being burnt than ever before.

As a result, we've produced so much carbon dioxide that levels are the highest they've been in 800,000 years!

We also produce another gas called methane. From farming – particularly cows, which burp methane.

These "greenhouse gases" occur naturally too – which is good, because without them Earth would be frozen and lifeless! But current levels are trapping too much heat in our atmosphere.

Lesson 3 Gaming safely

Activity 6.3a Reflection

You have learned about how to stay safe online while chatting or browsing. Another thing that we do online that brings other strangers into contact with us is gaming. Therefore, one needs to be careful if one needs to play video games online. What have you learned about keeping safe while playing online games?

In the clouds below, draw or write what you remember or what you would like more help with.

Lesson 3 Gaming safely

Activity 6.3b Online all the time

Read this extract from a book called *Hooked*.

10 o'clock The living room. There is an Alyssa-shaped hump under a blanket on the sofa and a glowing light. The door to the living room swings softly open and her dad looks in. He sees the hump and the glowing light.

DAD What on earth?

Dad steps forward and throws off the blanket.

Alyssa screams in shock.

ALYSSA Dad!! You gave me a heart attack!

DAD [very cross] What are you doing down here? You went to bed an HOUR ago!

ALYSSA I just wanted to finish something.

DAD [looking at the screen] You're watching videos!

ALYSSA They're teaching me how to build archways!

DAD I don't care, Alyssa, you should be asleep! I don't let you have your computer in your room at night for just this reason! I can't trust you. I had an email from your teacher today saying you hadn't done your homework for the past three weeks. You keep telling me you don't have any – it's a lie! I'm taking these.

He grabs the laptop and headphones.

Alyssa sighs

ALYSSA Fine. I'll finish it tomorrow.

DAD No, you won't. You're not having these back for a week.

ALYSSA WHAT??

DAD And you only get them back after that if you can show me some decent manners and catch up on your homework. And eat your dinner and go to bed on time.

ALYSSA Dad, you're totally over-reacting.

DAD Go back to bed, Alyssa.

Alyssa gets off the sofa and leaves the room, scowling.

Alyssa seems to be getting hooked on things she is watching online. This is a very easy trap to fall into.

If Alyssa was your friend, what would you suggest she could do to break her bad habit?

Unit reflection

What three things do you know about keeping safe now that you have completed this unit?

Is there anything you don't understand or want to learn more about?

Unit 5.7 Changing and learning

What do you know?

- What's happening in this image?
- How can we relate this to our lives?

In this unit, you will:

- Think about how we can change.
- Explore how mistakes can be a good thing.
- Think about how we can think.

Lesson 1 Changes

Activity 7.1a Changes

There are two columns below. Write a list of all the good things you can think of to do with change in the left column, and write all the harder aspects of change that you can think of in the right column.

What's good about change?	What's not so good about change?
• ____________________	• ____________________
• ____________________	• ____________________
• ____________________	• ____________________
• ____________________	• ____________________
• ____________________	• ____________________

Lesson 1 Changes

Activity 7.1b Poetry notes

As you have seen, change in inevitable. But big changes do not always have to be uncomfortable. Think of the image before where you saw the caterpillar changing into a beautiful butterfly. Change allows us to grow and improve upon ourselves. It also helps us to adapt to different situations. Reflect on a big change and note down your feelings about it below in the form of a non-rhyming poem.

Lesson 2 Problems waiting to be solved

Activity 7.2a Problems waiting to be solved

All of these items below were invented by mistake.

You are going to work with a friend or sibling and find out how these everyday objects came to be. You can either search for it online, or ask an adult. But remember to verify your research.

Object
1. Chocolate chip cookies
2. Penicillin
3. Cornflakes
4. Playdough
5. Dry cleaning

Object
6. Tyre (vulcanised) rubber
7. Safety pin
8. Crisps (potato chips)
9. Sticky notes
10. Matches

For each one you need to find out:

a) How it was invented (What is the story?)

b) Who invented it and when.

You can present your findings to the adults in your family however you would like.

If you have found out about all of these and still have time, see if you can find out about any more everyday items.

Lesson 2 Problems waiting to be solved

Activity 7.2b Reflection

Read this quote by Sir James Dyson, inventor of the bagless vaccum cleaner, about mistakes: "Successes teach you nothing. Failures teach you everything. Making mistakes is the most important thing you can do." How can knowing about how everyday objects came about due to mistakes help you when you make mistakes?

Write or draw your thoughts here.

Lesson 3 Brains into action

Activity 7.3a Brain into action plan

- What do I need to do? (assessment)
- What bit can I do well/not so well?
- What can help me? (Any practical resources?)
- How am I going to do it? (This is where you can write a list, sketch some ideas or do a visualisation.)
- Let's start!
- How am I doing? What's going well? Is there anything I need to change?
- When finished, ask: How did I do? (reflection) What went well? What do I need to improve? What can help me?

As you read before, metacognition helps us think about the ways in which we come up with ideas, and practising it can help us think better and quicker. While you have learnt visualisation, there are other simple tools we can use to get our brains all ready and firing. Go through the list above and use these questions to get started on your projects and tasks. Ask your guardian or an adult family member to give you a project or a chore, and use these questions to figure it out. Use the list above to help you when you are doing your brain games in this lesson.

When you have finished, use this space to write down what went well with using the list and what you want to work on.

Remember, this is a skill and, like any skill, the more you practise, the better you get.

Lesson 3 Brains into action

Activity 7.3b Notes

Unit reflection

Think about everything you have learned in this unit, then look again at this image from the introduction.

Imagine this butterfly is worried about the changes that are happening to it. What would you say to this butterfly to help it to change at each stage of its five stages from caterpillar to butterfly?

Unit 5.8 The environment

What do you know?

- Look at the picture of this building. Have you heard of the United Nations? If so, what do you know about it?
- What is sustainable development?
- What environmental issues are you aware of?
- What do you already do to help the planet?

In this unit, you will:

- Learn about waste.
- Think about our environmental impact on the planet.

Lesson 1 What can we do to make the world more sustainable?

Activity 8.1a My space for memories and photos!

With your friends or in your class, organise a 'Swap Day'. Everyone brings with them things like toys, books, or stationery that they're happy to swap for something else. One object can be swapped for only a similar object. Make sure that you have a trusted adult to help in the exchange, and also to explain reusing and recycling. Stick photos of your swap day on the cork board below.

Lesson 1 What can we do to make the world more sustainable?

Activity 8.1b Reflection

You had a swap day. What all did you learn from it? And what have you learned about the connection between recycling and sustainability so far? Watch a video with your guardian that contains the 17 sustainability goals as laid out by the UN to improve your understanding. Share this with your friends too. Share your thoughts on the actions you have taken towards living more sustainably.

How was the experience? What did you learn? How did you feel? What more can you do in your own life to support the sustainable goals?

Lesson 2 The Great Pacific Garbage Patch

Activity 8.2a Video notes

While watching 'The Great Pacific Garbage Patch' video, use this page to write notes and facts from the film.

Lesson 2 The Great Pacific Garbage Patch

Activity 8.2b Research

Using the internet, answer these questions about the Great Pacific Garbage Patch.

1. How big is the Great Pacific Garbage Patch?

____

____

2. How much plastic is there estimated to be in this garbage patch?

____

____

3. What are the main types of plastic found?

____

____

____

4. Where does the plastic come from?

____

____

____

5. What creatures live among the garbage?

____

____

____

6. Tell me any other interesting facts about the Great Pacific Garbage Patch.

____

____

____

Lesson 3 To travel or not to travel?

Activity 8.3a Debate notes

One of the biggest components of most pollutants is carbon. While carbon is completely safe by itself, it becomes harmful when in combination with other compounds and elements. To measure the cumulative pollution of a place, person, product or company, the term carbon footprint is used, which is the total pollutants that the place, person, product or company gives out.

Among the more polluting activities that contribute to our carbon footprint is air travel. While it is sometimes very necessary to be somewhere, the increasing aeroplane use all over the world is causing a lot of pollution. With a friend or a sibling, have a debate regarding whether we should travel or not travel to save the planet. Pick a side, and write down your debate notes here. What were the arguments for and against in your debate?

What do you think?

Lesson 3 To travel or not to travel?

Activity 8.3b Challenge: Can you draw the planet?

Unit reflection

In this unit you have learned about doing your bit for sustainability, about the Great Pacific Garbage Patch and you have debated the pros and cons of travelling.

Reflect back on this learning and, below, write or draw and label the key things you have learned.

Is there anything else you would like to learn or do not understand? Write these down.

Wellbeing for kids

Making kids smarter, happier

STAGE 6

Hello and welcome to Wellbeing Stage 6!

Dealing with feelings

Despite the exciting times ahead you probably have all sorts of feelings going on and these might feel quite mixed up. You might be a bit excited about the changes ahead, but you might feel nervous too. Perhaps you feel ready to move on, but worried about making new friends?

Never fear, this workbook is here to help you.

It will help you to name and understand your feelings and it will help you learn ways to feel calmer and more in control.

Exercising your mind

You do Physical Education every week at school to make your body strong and healthy. Physical exercise can help you do lots of things well (like dance and lift and heal).

When you do emotional exercises like the ones in this workbook, the same thing happens: you will also get stronger but in your mind, rather than in your body.

When you exercise your mind, you get better at things like managing your feelings. You also begin to find solving problems easier and learn to bounce back when things go wrong.

Mind exercises are amazing, and they are scientifically PROVEN to work.

Power tools!

This wellbeing workbook is powerful!

It will teach you all sorts of things that will help you in life, such as how to:

- calm yourself down
- cheer yourself up
- ask for help
- stand up for yourself
- get on well with others
- worry less
- feel happier more often
- handle feeling stressed.

Once you know how, you will see that you can change how you think, how you feel and how you act all by yourself.

It feels brilliant to be able to help yourself. And once you have learned how, you will be able to handle whatever comes your way with a lot more confidence.

Emotional health tools are power tools that you can use your whole life – whenever you need them.

Doesn't that sound brilliant?

If you are ready, then let's make a start!

May your year ahead be as special as you are!

– *Becky Goddard-Hill*

Unit 6.1 Our emotions

What do you know?

- What might be happening in the picture?
- How might the child be feeling?
- How might she react to this?

In this unit, you will:

- Explore people's reactions to emotions.
- Consider a range of scenarios and how each character might feel and react.
- Create a booklet which gives information about the causes of stress and includes strategies to overcome it.

Lesson 1 Exploring emotions

Activity 1.1 How might they feel and react?

Look at each of the scenarios below. How might each of the characters be feeling? How might they react in these situations?

1.

Charlize and her dad planned to go swimming at the weekend. Charlize has been looking forward to it all week, but on Saturday morning, her dad gets called into work and he has to cancel the swimming. What emotions might Charlize be feeling? What emotions might her dad be feeling?

How might Charlize feel?

____

____

How might her dad feel?

____

____

2.

Paulo and his brother have just been told that they are going to a theme park. Paulo doesn't like rollercoasters, but he does love the characters and the food stalls. What emotions do you think he and his brother might be feeling?

How might Paulo feel?

____

____

How might his brother feel?

____

____

3.

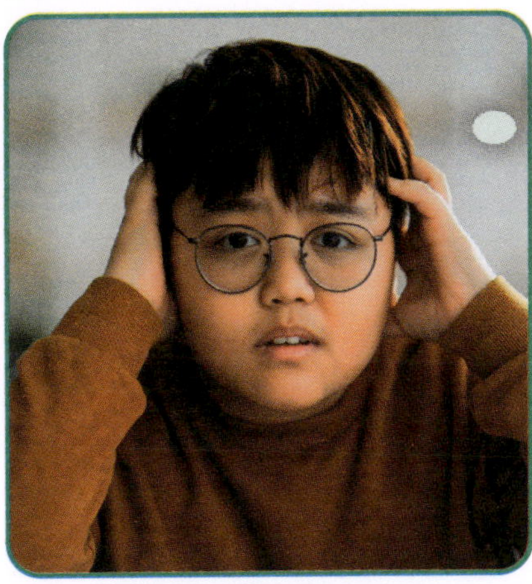

Jeno has fallen out with his best friend. He has just texted him but his friend isn't replying. What emotions do you think Jeno is feeling?

How might Jeno feel?

____

____

How might his friend feel?

____

____

Lesson 2 How stress can affect our bodies

Activity 1.2a What is stress?

Draw a picture that represents stress. You can use colour, shape, scenarios or words to explore what stress is.

Lesson 2 How stress can affect our bodies

Activity 1.2b What might make people feel stressed?

Stress is a state of worry, where we either have mental tension about something that is happening, or something that could go wrong. It is a natural response of the mind to concentrate on the things that require our urgent attention. But sometimes, it can be harmful too, and can have short and long term effects on one's mood and body.

Have you ever felt stressed? What made you feel this way?

What other things might cause people to feel stressed?

Lesson 3 Feeling worried

Activity 1.3a Times of change

You have seen how big and small changes alike can affect your mood. A change that is about to happen soon might also cause us stress and worry. And depending on our age, our sources of worry differ from person to person. What worries might students of your age have?

What advice would you give?

Choose one worry and create an advice page for students on how they could overcome this worry.

Lesson 3 Feeling worried

Activity 1.3b Reflection

Consider the emotions below and think about times when you have experienced each emotion or feeling. Complete the sentences below.

I feel happy when ______________________________

I feel excited when ______________________________

I feel overwhelmed when ______________________________

I feel scared when ______________________________

I feel hopeful when ______________________________

I feel angry when ______________________________

Unit reflection

Think about your lessons from this unit. Consider three key things you have learned and write them below.

1. ______________________________

____

2. ______________________________

____

3. ______________________________

____

What strategies might you use to calm down when you feel stressed? Make a mind map below.

Unit 6.2 Healthy minds

What do you know?

- What can you see in the photo?
- How might the man be feeling?

In this unit, you will:

- Discuss why it is important to relax.
- Take part in a debate about editing photos.
- Create a class exercise book.

Lesson 1 Self-care

Activity 2.1a What is your day like?

Fill in your daily schedule on this 24-hour diary. Be honest – no one is judging you.

Time (24-hr)	Activity	How does this activity make you feel?
00:00		
01:00		
02:00		
03:00		
04:00		
05:00		
06:00		
07:00		
08:00		
09:00		
10:00		
11:00		
12:00		
13:00		
14:00		
15:00		
16:00		
17:00		
18:00		
19:00		
20:00		
21:00		
22:00		
23:00		

Lesson 1 Self-care

Activity 2.1b How do you like to relax?

One of the ways to practise self care is by engaging in relaxation. Try all of these relaxing activities and answer the questions below.

1. Clay modelling or sand sculpting
2. Doodling and colouring in a sketchbook
3. Listening to classical music with closed eyes.

Which ones did you like?

What other ways of relaxing do you enjoy?

Why is it important for us to relax?

Lesson 2 Comparing yourself with others

Activity 2.2a Photoshopping

Should it be made illegal to photoshop images which are posted online or used in advertising?

What are your thoughts? Write your ideas below.

Lesson 2 Comparing yourself with others

Activity 2.2b The big debate!

You have now read about comparisons and how photoshopping images is common online. Now it's time for another debate. Making two teams of your friends and family members, debate the either side of this question: Should photoshopping of images of people's bodies be banned online and in advertising? Use the space below to plan your debate. Make a note of your research points and which websites or books you used to find your information.

Lesson 3 What is so good about exercise and movement?

Activity 2.3a Instructions for great exercise

You are going to create a page for a class book called 'Our Favourite Ways to Exercise'.

1. Think of something that you love doing that will help your friends get fit.

2. Write or draw clear instructions to help them.

(You will need to include details such as whether they will need an adult with them, where it is going to take place, what they might need and how long it will take.)

My exercise:

Lesson 3 What is so good about exercise and movement?

Activity 2.3b Reflections

Consider what you have learned about exercise and movement in your lesson. Do you think that the effect of exercise can be similar to that of relaxation, in that it makes a person feel positive? Many forms of exercise and activity involve being outside, which is good for our vitamin D levels and also to get some fresh air or a change of scenery; exercise and movement can give us a break from school work or other things throughout the day and allow us time to express our energy in a different way; physical movement can produce happy hormones called endorphins. It can be a way to socialise with others.

What are three key things you have learned?

1. ______________________________

2. ______________________________

3. ______________________________

Unit reflection

Take some time to really think about what you have learned over this unit.

What have you learned about the importance of taking time to relax, and strategies you can use to relax and feel mentally healthy?

Draw or write some interesting facts or reflections below. Are there any strategies which you might try to include in your day-to-day life to support your own healthy mind?

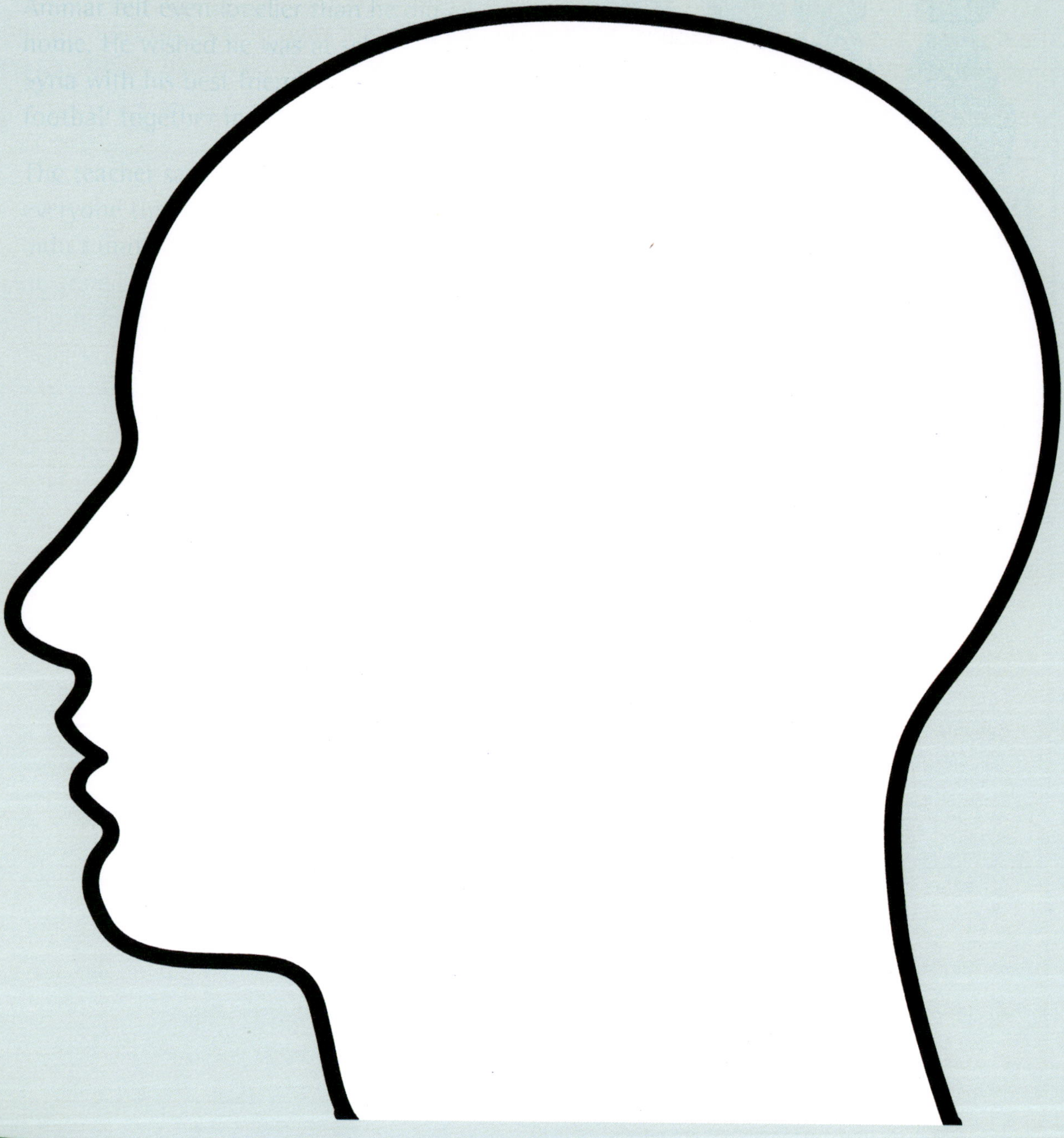

Unit 6.3 Medicines and health

What do you know?

- What is happening in the picture?
- How do you think each of the characters feel?

In this unit, you will:

- Create a poster of how you can support a friend who might be feeling down or be struggling with their mental health.
- Describe what medicines do and how they can be used safely.
- Create an information leaflet about how vaccinations work and why they are administered.

Lesson 1 What to do if I'm worried

Activity 3.1 Supporting a friend in need

Write down all the strategies which you might use to support a friend who is struggling with their mental health or feeling down.

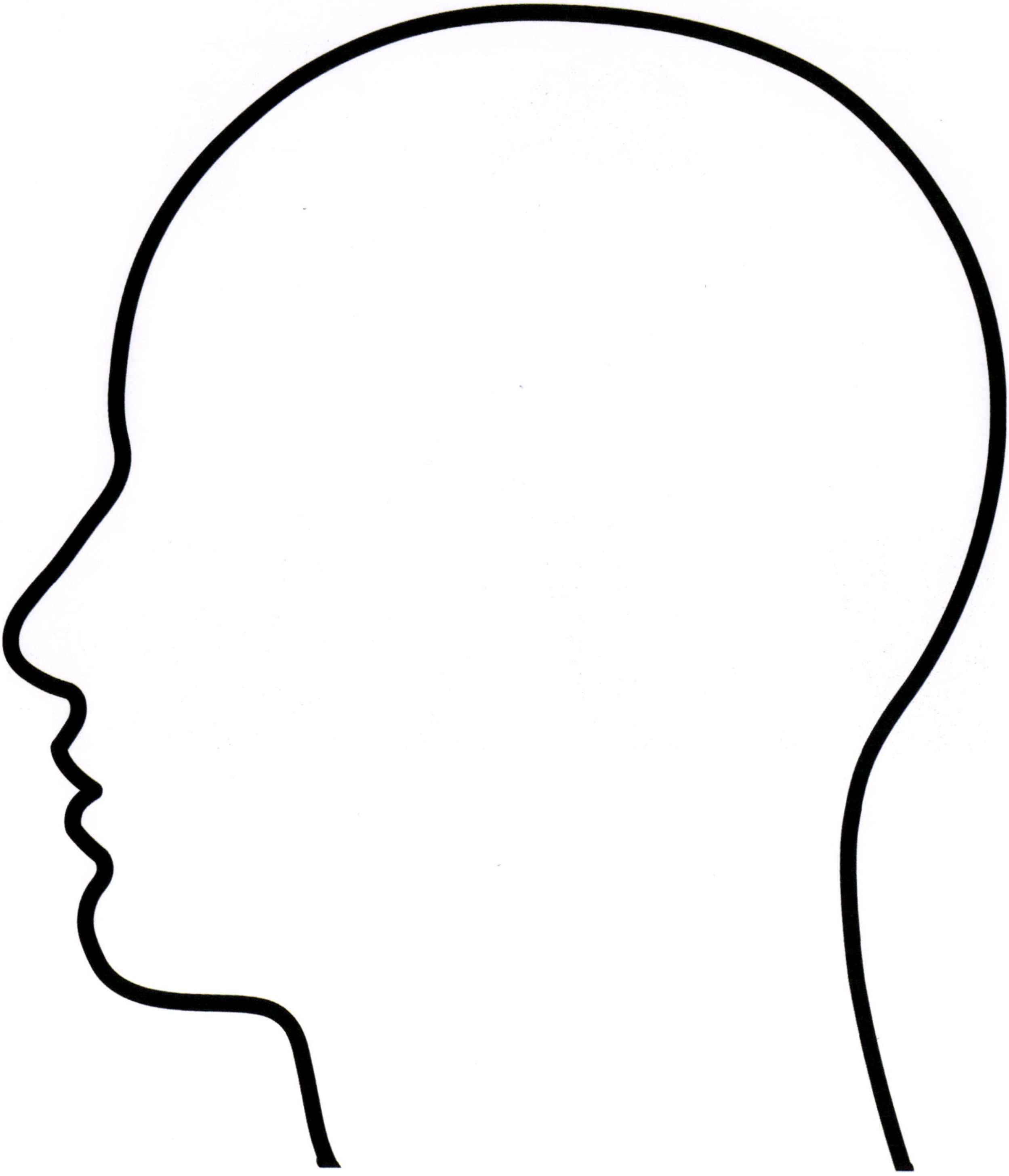

Lesson 2 Medicines and health

Activity 3.2a What should they do?

Read each of the scenarios and advise the characters on what they should do.

Max is at his grandma's house. He has a headache and wants to take some medicine to help it. He sees the medicine he is looking for. He doesn't want to bother his grandma as she is busy, so he thinks he should just take it himself. What should Max do?

Priah finds some tablets on the kitchen floor. What should she do?

Ajeet has a sore throat, so his friend offers him some of his throat syrup. What should Ajeet do?

Lesson 2 Medicines and health

Activity 3.2b Medicines quiz

Research the answers to the questions on your own or with your friends or siblings.

1. Who discovered antibiotics?

2. What does an antiseptic do?

3. List three safety rules when storing or taking medicines.

4. What should you do if someone other than a trusted adult offers you drugs or medicine?

5. Tablets are the only form of medicine. True or false? Explain your answer.

Lesson 2 Medicines and health

Activity 3.2c Antibiotics

Read the extract below from the book *Surgery Through Time* to learn more about antibiotics today and answer the questions below in groups.

We now have many different antibiotics, used to kill different bacteria. But some bacteria are changing and are no longer killed by existing antibiotics. Scientists constantly look for new antibiotics.

Keeping hospitals very clean is even more important as antibiotics work better in clean conditions. Medical staff scrub themselves with soap and wear sterile clothes. Instruments are sterilised by boiling or radiation, and surfaces are all cleaned thoroughly with antiseptics.

– *Anne Rooney*

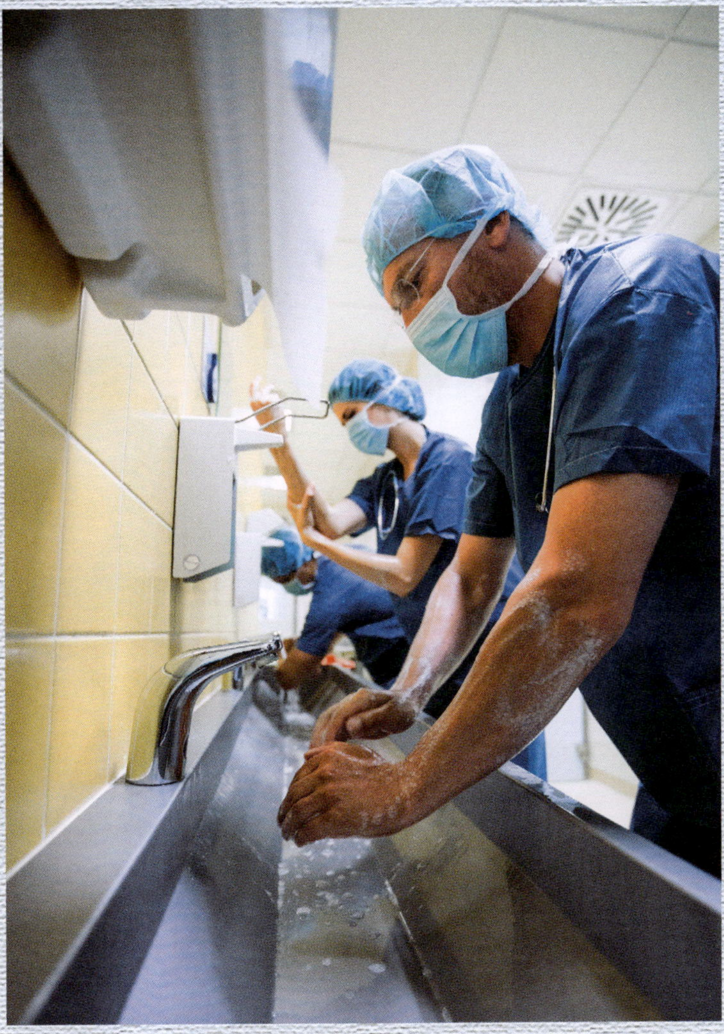

Consider and discuss these questions with your family members.

1. How do you think antibiotics differ now from when they were discovered?
2. Why is it important that hospitals are clean and what do you think staff have to do to ensure that they are clean?
3. Why are scientists always looking for new antibiotics?

Lesson 3 Vaccinations

Activity 3.3a Edward Jenner fact file

Find out facts about Edward Jenner, his personal and professional life. Consider where and when he lived, what he studied and how he discovered vaccines.

Lesson 3 Vaccinations

Activity 3.3b Vaccination facts

List as many facts about vaccinations as you can below. Share these with your family and friends. Did any one have facts that you didn't?

Unit reflection

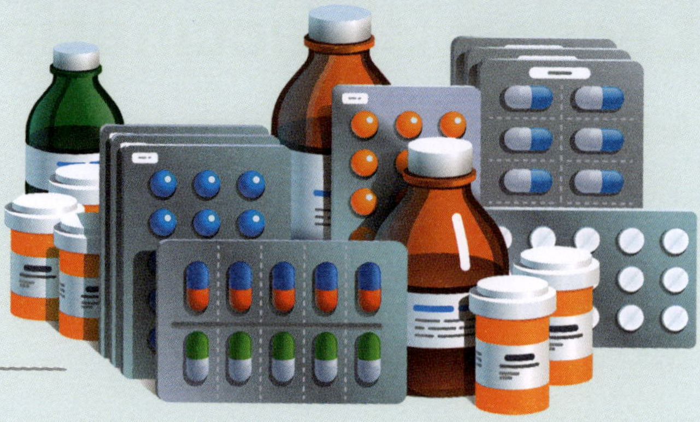

Consider what you have learned in this unit. Write your reflections below.

1. What are medicines?

2. What can they do?

3. How can we keep medicines safe?

4. Who could you go to if you were worried about the health of a friend?

Unit 6.4 People and me

What do you know?

- What's happening with the toddlers in this picture?
- If you were their big sister or brother, how would you get them to resolve their conflict?

In this unit, you will:

- Consider stereotypes and how we can challenge them.
- Learn about conflict resolution.
- Find out about the six different types of peer pressure.

Lesson 1 Stereotypes

Activity 4.1a What do I know?

Everything I think
I know about stereotypes

Lesson 1 Stereotypes

Activity 4.1b Reflection

Now that you have written down what you thought of stereotypes, look up the word's definition in a dictionary. Stereotyping is a form of snap judgement that we make about people around us. What do you think is wrong about stereotyping? And are there any situations where it is acceptable? Talk to your guardian, and try thinking of a time when you made a snap judgement about someone based on their looks or the way they talked. Was it the right thing to do? What did you learn or begin to think about from this activity?

Write down everything you remember and rank the points in order of importance to you with number 1 being the least important.

1. ______________________________

____

____

____

2. ______________________________

____

____

____

3. ______________________________

____

____

____

4. ______________________________

____

____

____

5. ______________________________

____

____

____

Lesson 2 When we fall out

Activity 4.2a When we fall out

Read this story about a family.

'I hate you!' shouted Najeeb as he slammed his bedroom door and flung himself on his bed. His little sister was SOOOOO stupid! He could hear her crying loudly downstairs.

The door opened and his mum came in. 'Habib Albi, what has got into you? Your sister is so sad! This is not like you!'

Mum sat down on his bed and waited for him to talk.

Najeeb started to cry – he felt angry and sad all at once. He knew it wasn't like him. He loved his little sister, Kyra; she was funny and sweet, and they were normally good friends.

He told his mum how she was running around in the living room being silly and she had fallen over him and broken his model – the one he had nearly finished after working on it for months. She had hurt herself, but Najeeb hadn't cared... He had felt so cross with her that he had shouted really loudly in her face and pushed her roughly out the way and then she had screamed back at him.

Mum understood why Najeeb was so upset but she wasn't happy with how he had reacted. She told him to calm down and then they would talk about it all together...

Talk to an adult family member and write down your answers.

Why did Najeeb and Kyra fall out?

____

____

How did they act towards one another when they were hurt and angry?

____

____

What can they do to sort it out?

____

____

Lesson 2 When we fall out

Activity 4.2b When we fall out

You have read about the falling out between Najeeb and Kyra. Now, think about the conversation they would have with their mum. How would they talk, and what would their body language be like? And how different would it be once they have spoken with their mum and calmed down?

Afterwards, answer the questions below.

1. What have I learned today?

2. Can I list all the positive things people can do when they fall out?

3. What can I change or try next time I fall out with someone?

Lesson 3 Under pressure

Activity 4.3a Your pressure relief doodle page

Lesson 3 Under pressure

Activity 4.3b Reflection

Now that you have learned a bit about peer pressure, answer the questions below. You can seek the help of a trusted adult to complete these.

1. What is peer pressure?

____

____

____

2. What were the six different types of peer pressure?

____

____

____

3. In what sort of situations might we experience peer pressure? Write some examples.

____

____

____

4. What strategies could you use if you felt you were being pressured to do something you didn't want to do?

____

____

____

5. Is there anything that has worried you or you would like to learn more about regarding peer pressure?

____

____

____

Unit reflection

Reflect back to the unit introduction and revisit the question, "If you were the toddlers' big sister or brother, how would you get them to resolve their conflict?"

Read back over how you answered that question and ask yourself if you would change anything you wrote and, if so, what?

Use the space below to write what you would do and say now.

Unit 6.5 Community and choices

What do you know?

- What can you see in the picture?
- What do you think is happening?
- Who is involved in the picture?

In this unit, you will:

- Consider what your own boundaries are and how you can respect the boundaries of others.
- Create a map of the local community showing all of the community groups you belong to.
- Design a community centre which will benefit all local people.

Lesson 1 I have choices

Activity 5.1a Decisions, decisions

Consider choices that have been made in your life. How were these decisions made? Who made them? These can be any kind of decisions, big or small.

What is the decision?	Who makes the decision?	Why do they make the decision?

Lesson1 I have choices

Activity 5.1b Personal boundaries

With an adult, discuss and look up the meaning of the words boundaries, permission and choices. Ask them about the concept of personal space. After your discussion, try writing or drawing the ending for each scenario.

Write or draw an ending for each scenario.

Alice and Maria are sitting on the carpet in the classroom, listening to the teacher. Alice keeps playing with Maria's hair and she doesn't like it, but she doesn't want to be rude. What could she do?

Devon is at a family party and is about to leave with his family. His mum wants him to hug his Aunty Sandra goodbye, but he doesn't want to. What should he do?

Jamil and Max are playing together in the playground. Jamil wants to stand very close to Max, but Max keeps moving away. What should Max do?

Lesson 2 I belong to my community

Activity 5.2 Community map

Work with your friends or siblings to consider all of the communities you belong to. These might be sport teams, music groups, places of worship and so on. Draw or write about each one below.

Communities I belong to

Lesson 3 It's everyone's community

Activity 5.3 Design task

Design a community centre or space which would benefit everyone. With the help of a trusted adult and few friends, you can also make your own 3D model of it with cardboard and thermocol. Identify all of the key features of your community centre on the next page.

Write all of the key design features of your community centre or space below.

Unit reflection

Spend some time reflecting on what community means to you. Can you think of some words connected with community? These might be words which link to how being part of a community makes you feel, what communities can do or different types of communities. Write words starting with the first letter of the word community below.

C ______________________________

O ______________________________

M ______________________________

M ______________________________

U ______________________________

N ______________________________

I ______________________________

T ______________________________

Y ______________________________

Now spend some time reflecting on what decisions are yours to make, and why, when you are younger, other people make some decisions for you.

Unit 6.6 Our safety

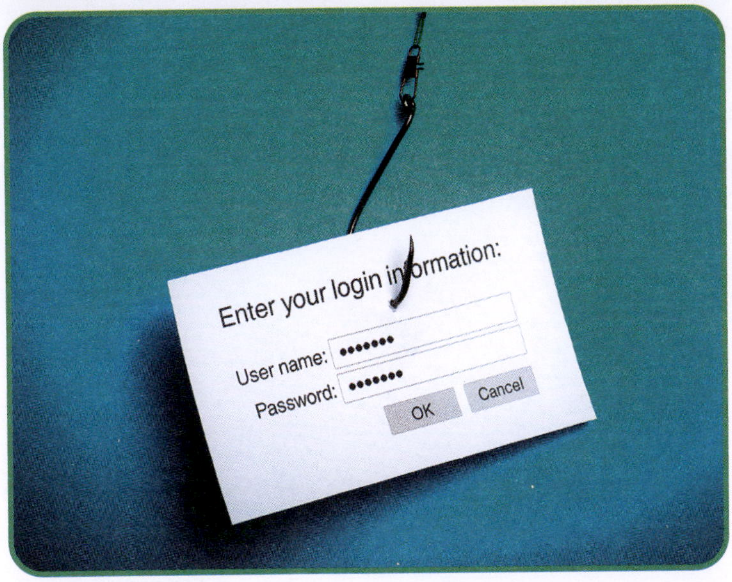

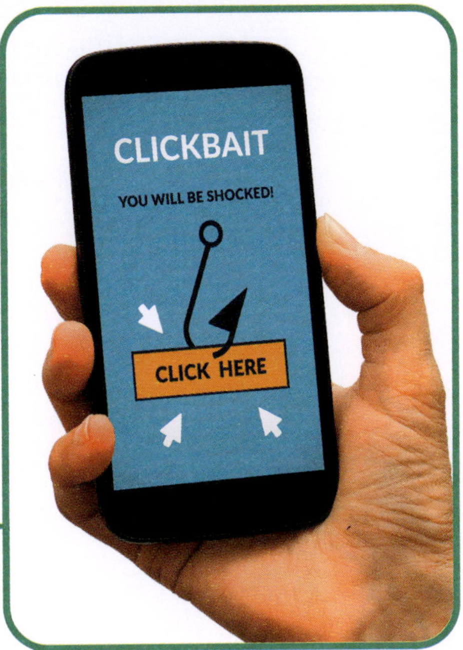

What do you know?

- What do we need passwords and PINs for?
- What do you think clickbait is? Draw what you think it is. (If you don't know, have a guess!)

In this unit, you will:

- Learn about passwords and PINs.
- Learn about clickbait.
- Learn about first aid.

Lesson 1 PINs and passwords

Activity 6.1 Designing passwords

See how many different unique passwords you can design below. One has been done for you: sUntrE!e4Brick. This has been made using three random words: sun, tree and brick. There are lower-case and upper-case letters and two characters (! and 4) mixed in to make it more complex.

Now it's your turn! How many can you make?

- ______________________________
- ______________________________
- ______________________________
- ______________________________
- ______________________________
- ______________________________
- ______________________________
- ______________________________

Lesson 2 First aid

Activity 6.2a What can I do to help?

Are you familiar with first aid? Have you ever received it? Look up online and discuss with an adult when first aid can be given, and when it is suitable to wait for a trained medical professional instead. Choose one of the common first aid situations and research how you can help a patient in this situation.

I am researching how to help someone who

I need to

What else do I need to think about?

Lesson 2 First aid

Lesson 6.2b The recovery position

Look at these images and steps about how to help a person who has fallen unconscious. With an adult, enact these steps to understand them better.

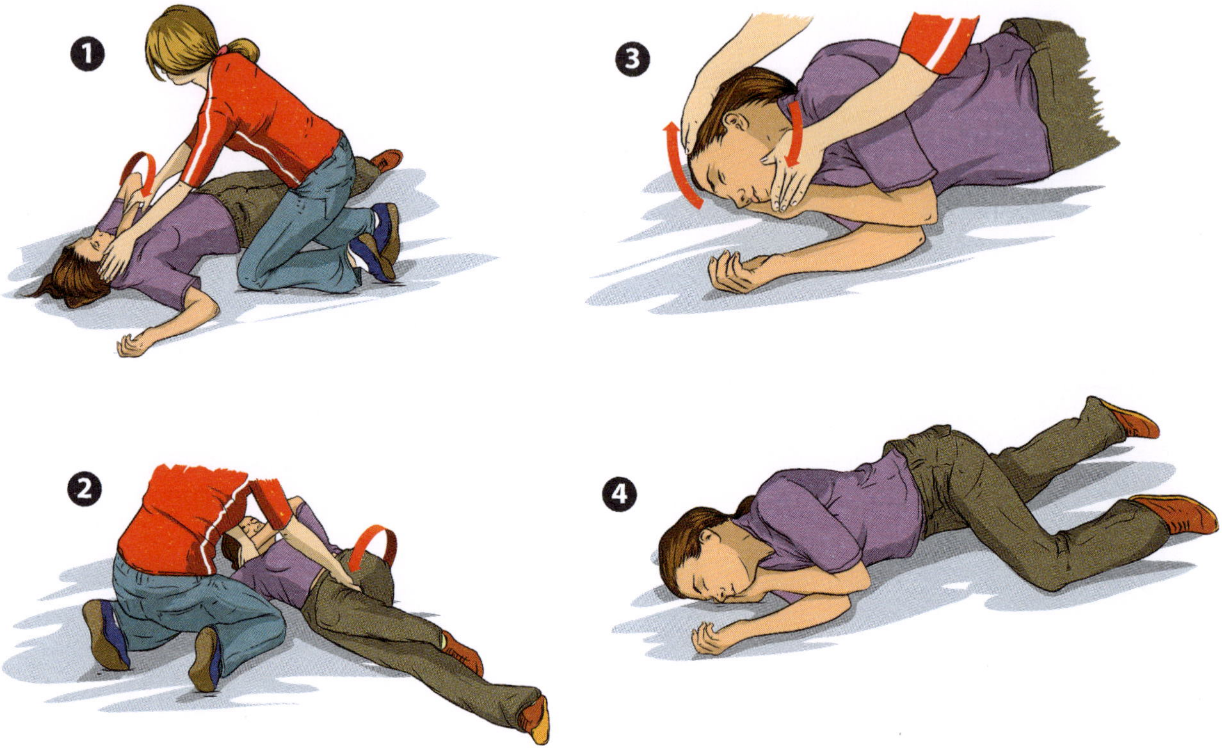

- With the patient lying on their back, place the nearest arm to you at a right angle to their body.
- Move the other arm across the chest with the back of the hand underneath the patient's cheek.
- Bend the leg furthest away, bringing it towards you until the foot is flat on the floor.
- Holding the bent leg and with your hand underneath the patient's cheek, roll the patient onto their side.
- Tilt their head back to open their airways.

Lesson 2 First aid

Lesson 6.2c The role of a paramedic

Read the extract below from *Dani Binns Practical Paramedic* to learn more about the role of a paramedic.

"What happened?" Dani asked the boy.

"She was riding into the park, quite fast. She swerved to avoid me and flew over the handlebars. I think she landed on her head. I told her not to move. Then I called for an ambulance," he replied.

"You did the right thing, telling her not to move," said Tai. "If she landed on her head, she might have injured her neck or back. That's very serious."

Asha checked the girl's pulse and breathing. Then she put an inflating cuff around the girl's arm to check her blood pressure. Tai shone a mini torch in her eyes to check her reactions.

Have you learned anything useful from reading this extract? If so, what is it?

Lesson 3 Clickbait

Activity 6.3a Clickbait

Would you be tempted to click on any of these? Why? What words do they use to draw you in? Discuss this with a trusted adult, then circle the words and add notes to show all the strategies they use to tempt people to click to take you to their web page.

Lesson 3 Clickbait

Activity 6.3b The dangers of clickbait

Now that you have seen the dangers of clickbait, how about you try your hand at creating your own clickbait ad? However, instead of getting people to click on it, create a clickbait ad that shows the dangers of it! What kind of words and images would you use?

Home About Offers Contact

http://www.do_not_trust.com

FREE upgrade to the latest smartphone!

CLICK HERE To get your FREE new phone tomorrow! CLICK HERE

Unit reflection

What three things do you know now you have completed this unit?

Unit 6.7 Tackling the tough stuff

What do you know?

- What does this picture represent to you?
- How might life sometimes feel tough, like there is a storm cloud blocking out the sun?
- How can noticing the 'silver lining' help when you are in challenging times?

In this unit, you will:

- Consider how we deal with loss and change.
- Think about how we deal with mistakes.
- Think about how we can breeze exams!

Lesson 1 Moving

Activity 7.1a Top tips for moving

How could you make someone who is new to the country feel more welcome or settled?

Write down your top five strategies to support them.

1. ______________________________

2. ______________________________

3. ______________________________

4. ______________________________

5. ______________________________

Lesson 1 Moving

Activity 7.1b Interview questions

You will be interviewing staff within your school who have moved areas or countries. What questions would you like to ask them so that you have a better understanding of how people feel when they move? What helped them to feel more settled?

1. ______________________________
____
____
____

2. ______________________________
____
____
____

3. ______________________________
____
____
____

4. ______________________________
____
____
____

5. ______________________________
____
____
____
____

Lesson 2 Never give up

Activity 7.2a Practising and giving your best

Practice, determination and giving your best – this is what Michael Jordan's parents said were the things that would help to make him a winner. How can you apply this to your goals?

Draw a picture below of you achieving your goal. Around the outside of your picture.

Lesson 2 Never give up

Activity 7.2b Reflection

- After seeing Michael Jordan's story and what he says about making mistakes, Has it helped you to see mistakes in a different way? If so, how?

____

____

____

- Write or draw below all that you have learned, or what you now think about mistakes.

Lesson 3 Exams, I'm ready!

Activity 7.3a Metacognition

What do you remember about metacognition? Write or draw below what you have learned and how your metacognition journey is going. Have you noticed anything about your thinking or used any of the skills you have learned, such as visualisation?

Lesson 3 Exams, I'm ready!

Activity 7.3b Reflection

Exams can be a tough time, with all the subjects that have to be remembered. Think of your 'Brain in action plan' and other metacognition tools you learned about before. How can you use them to improve your performance here in exams?

Unit reflection: Relax

You've learned about how to tackle tricky things in this unit.

Here's a page to colour in and calm you if you are feeling anxious or worried, or just for fun, now or in the future. Enjoy!

Unit 6.8 The world we live in

What do you know?

- Look closely. What can you see in this picture?
- What do you love about our world? Draw all the things you love.

In this unit, you will:

- Learn about the 4 Rs of waste reduction.
- Understand what ethical consumerism is.
- Consider the beauty of our diverse world.

Lesson 1 What's the good news?

Activity 8.1a What I know

Create a mind map and write down everything you can think of to do with sustainability, sustainable development goals and the 4 Rs – Reduce, Recycle, Reuse, Repurpose. If you have any questions, you can write these in the space below.

Sustainability

Questions I have about sustainability issues:

Lesson 1 What's the good news?

Activity 8.1b A good news story

Create a 'Good News' newspaper on how people are following the 4 Rs in clever ways. Choose a news story about sustainability that inspired you and research it, then write an article in your own words. Go through the newspapers in your home to look at the different kinds of articles and headlines for ideas.

Daily **NEWS**

Lesson 2 Fairtrade

Activity 8.2a Fairtrade chocolate advert script

Lesson 2 Fairtrade

Activity 8.2b Fairtrade illustration

Draw an illustration below for a Fairtrade advert for newspapers and magazines or for public transport.

Lesson 3 Diverse communities

Activity 8.3a My interview

With the help of your guardian, interview your neighbours or new classmates to get to know them and their cultural background better. Write the questions you are going to ask in your interview. Try to find out as much as you can about the person's culture. For example, you could ask questions about language or dialect, history, race, food, music, religious beliefs, festivals and celebrations or anything else you wish to ask them.

(Use the back of the sheet if you need more room.)

1. ______________________________

2. ______________________________

3. ______________________________

4. ______________________________

5. ______________________________

6. ______________________________

Lesson 3 Diverse communities

Activity 8.3b Making a kinder world

If you were in charge of the world, what would you do to make it a kinder place for everyone to live in?

Unit reflection

What changes are you going to make in your life based on what you have learned in this unit?

Go back through your workbook to help you remember.

Acknowledgements

We are grateful to the following for permission to reproduce copyright material:

5.4.3, An extract about bullying, NSPCC, https://www.nspcc.org.uk/what-is-child-abuse/types-of-abuse/bullying-and-cyberbullying/. Reproduced with permission; **5.6.3**, "Game age ratings explained", PEGI, copyright © PEGI S.A. Reproduced with permission;

4.1.1 Vector bucket/ Shutterstock, StudioBrandShop/ Shutterstock, ober-art / Shutterstock, Vector bucket/ Shutterstock, jsabirova/Shutterstock, WS 4.1.1a jsabirova/Shutterstock, **4.1.2** WS 4.1.2b YASH GARG FOTOGRAFIE/Shutterstock, **4.1.3** MinskDesign/ Shutterstock, **4.2.2** Ealita.ID/ Shutterstock, Ealita.ID/ Shutterstock, Nicoleta Ionescu/Shutterstock, **4.2.3** WS Nicoleta Ionescu/Shutterstock, **4.3.1** WS 4.3.1a Jr images/ Shutterstock, RomanR/ Shutterstock, NIPAPORN PANYACHAROEN/ Shutterstock, MarcoFood/ Shutterstock, Tim UR/ Shutterstock, Ermak Oksana/ Shutterstock, Dionisvera/ Shutterstock, baibaz/ Shutterstock, Craevschii Family/ Shutterstock, New Africa/ Shutterstock, **4.3.2** Benjamin Ordaz/ Shutterstock, inspiring.team/ Shutterstock, **4.4.1** Monkey Business Images/Shutterstock, Rohit Seth/Shutterstock, Athanasia Nomikou/ Shutterstock, 4.**4.2** Athanasia Nomikou/ Shutterstock, **4.4.3** Svetliy/ Shutterstock, **4.5.1** dzejdi/ Shutterstock, IZZ HAZEL/ Shutterstock, nikolae/Shutterstock, TotemArt/ Shutterstock, **4.5.2** OlyaOK/ Shutterstock, Eightshot_Studio /Shutterstock, SB Eightshot_Studio / Shutterstock, **4.5.3** Luis Molinero/Shutterstock, **4.6.1** cunaplus/ Shutterstock, Dinesh Hukmani/ Shutterstock, Fedor Selivanov/ Shutterstock, Motortion Films/ Shutterstock, **4.6.3** hurricanehank/ Shutterstock, WS 4.6.3 hurricanehank/ Shutterstock, 4.7.1 ChristianChan / Shutterstock, **4.7.2** Zainudin_ Kho /Shutterstock, WS 4.7.2 Zainudin_Kho / **4.8.1** max dallocco/ Shutterstock, WS Studio_G/ Shutterstock, **4.8.2** © HarperCollins Publisher 2020, frank60/ Shutterstock, Rich Carey/ Shutterstock, Maryshot/ Shutterstock, **5.1.1** Atomic Roderick/ Shutterstock, Jasmine Creation/ Shutterstock, mentalmind/ Shutterstock, **5.1.3** HowLettery/Shutterstock, CallMeTak/ Shutterstock WS HowLettery/Shutterstock, **5.2.1** KlingSup/ Shutterstock, **5.2.2** karakotsya/ Shutterstock, **5.2.3** Viktorija Reuta/Shutterstock, Aleksandr Merg/ Shutterstock, WS 5.2.3a Aleksandr Merg/ Shutterstock, woocat/ Shutterstock, woocat/ Shutterstock, WS 5.2.3b, Viktorija Reuta/Shutterstock, **5.3.1** pixelheadphoto digitalskillet/ Shutterstock, F01 PHOTO/ Shutterstock, fizkes/ Shutterstock fSB PixyPen/ Shutterstock, Colorfuel Studio/ Shutterstock, **5.4.1** Rawpixel.com/ Shutterstock, Vegorus/Shutterstock, WS Vegorus/ Shutterstock,Monkey Business Images/ Shutterstock, **5.4.2** afry_harvy/ Shutterstock, Reprinted by permission of HarperCollins Publishers Ltd © 2022 A. M. Dassu, **5.5.1** SewCreamStudio/Shutterstock, **5.5.3** Elena Zajchikova/ Shutterstock, Victoria 1/ Shutterstock, Maksym Drozd/ Shutterstock, **5.6.1** WESTOCK PRODUCTIONS/ Shutterstock, Pungu x/ Shutterstock, WS Pungu x/ Shutterstock, **5.6.2** TR STOK/ Shutterstock, Gatien GREGORI/Shutterstock, Text Reprinted by permission of HarperCollins Publishers Ltd © 2022 Mio Debnam, **5.6.3** Reprinted by permission of HarperCollins Publishers Ltd © 2023 Jo Cotterill, Monster Ztudio/ Shutterstock, Rafael Croonen/ Shutterstock, Luce Altra/ Shutterstock, **5.7.1** Darkdiamond67/ Shutterstock, **5.7.2** SB p.53 GoodStudio/ Shutterstock, **5.8.1** SB p.57 nexus 7/ Shutterstock, p.58 piotr_pabijan/ Shutterstock, **5.8.2** Shane Gross/ Shutterstock, **5.8.3** BearFotos/Shutterstock, WS BearFotos/ Shutterstock, Dmitrijs Mihejevs/ Shutterstock, **6.1.1** F01 PHOTO/ Shutterstock, Asti Mak/ Shutterstock, Roman Samborskyi/ Shutterstock, Prostock-studio/ Shutterstock, Dmytro Onopko/ Shutterstock, **6.1.2** JPC-PROD/Shutterstock, Veja/ Shutterstock, **6.1.3** Vector bucket/ Shutterstock, Yayayoyo/ Shutterstock, Dmytro Onopko/ Shutterstock, IYIKON/ Shutterstock, **6.2.1** Dejan Dundjerski/ Shutterstock, Brian A Jackson/ Shutterstock, Arcady/ Shutterstock, Yuganov Konstantin/Shutterstock, **6.2.2** T. Lesia/ Shutterstock, **6.2.3** Zoart Studio/ Shutterstock,Vitalii Petrenko/Shutterstock, WS 6.3.1 Zoart Studio/ Shutterstock, **6.3.1** Zoart Studio/ Shutterstock, Jeruik/ Shutterstock, **6.3.2** Iconic Bestiary/ Shutterstock, wavebreakmedia/ Shutterstock, **6.3.3** UnderhilStudio/ Shutterstock, Oxy_gen/Shutterstock , WS 6.3.3 UnderhilStudio/ Shutterstock, **6.4.1** AMR Studio/ Shutterstock, **6.4.3** Nata Bene/ Shutterstock, **6.5.1** Rawpixel.com/ Shutterstock, Rudie Strummer/ Shutterstock, **6.5.3** Nizwa Design/ Shutterstock, **6.6.1** Antlii/ Shutterstock, maicasaa/ Shutterstock, omphoto/ Shutterstock, Vitalii Vodolazskyi/Shutterstock, WS 6.6.1 Vitalii Vodolazskyi/ Shutterstock, **6.6.2** EreborMountain/Shutterstock, Reprinted by permission of HarperCollins Publishers Ltd © 2020 Lisa Rajan, **6.6.3** desdemona72/ Shutterstock, **6.7.1** Jacques Paganel/ Shutterstock, Vasilinka/ Shutterstock, Bibadash/ Shutterstock, Simakova Mariia/ Shutterstock, WS 6.7.1, **6.7.3** Christina Designs/ Shutterstock, **6.8.1** Nostalgia for Infi nity/ Shutterstock, **6.8.3** Lightspring/ Shutterstock, phloxii/ Shutterstock, WS 6.8.2 Simakova Mariia/ Shutterstock

All additional text reprinted by permission of HarperCollins Publishers Ltd © 2024.

The Wellbeing for Kids Series